FOOTPRINTS

FOOTPRINTS

The True Story Behind the Poem

That Inspired Millions

Updated Edition

MARGARET FISHBACK POWERS

Collins

To my husband, Paul, with love and appreciation
for a wonderful life and partnership.

To our four distinctively different and creative
grandchildren: Paige, Max (Mackenzie Barclay), Calvin,
and Corinna. You continue to sculpt meaningful memories
for our memory bank and will no doubt make an
impact on the world . . . for all things good.

To the many boys and girls around the globe with whom we
have shared our message of hope and love.
We have become forever friends.

And to four special lifetime family friends: Betty Reside,
Shirley Reside, Eleanor Côté, and Volie Grover. You are like
four brightly blooming flowers in our garden of love.

Contents

FOOTPRINTS

Foreword

Several years ago, while we were living in Andover, England, we were given Margaret Fishback Powers' book about the story behind the "Footprints" poem. Her story touched our lives so deeply that we could not put the book down until we had read the last word. As we were reading, we learned that our families have been intertwined down through the decades. Paul had been in bible college in London, Ontario, with David's father, Rev. Roland Smith. Paul and Margaret had been coming to England for seventeen years, but we had never met. So we contacted them and invited them to visit us in Andover. Since that time, we have continued on almost a yearly basis to minister together in Europe, Canada, and the Caribbean islands. We have personally seen tens of thousands of lives changed, blessed, and encouraged through their ministry. Their testimony does not sugarcoat the tough realities of life, but they have demonstrated that no matter what challenge they face, God will always be there to uphold them.

God is the creator and sustainer of our lives, and He cares for His children through the storms of life. Everyone needs to rely on someone to carry them during the fragile times of life. We are all carried for up to nine months in our mother's womb. Then, until we can walk, we are carried everywhere. When we are sick, we rely on others to carry us to places of care and recovery. God's sustaining care for us is similar to a parent carrying a child or to a shepherd carrying his sheep. God cradles us in His loving arms. Sometimes we cannot make sense of life, but even in the confusion God is still there to hold us. We may not understand it all now, but one day we will look back and know that He is the one who carried us through it all.

We have had the opportunity to observe Paul and

Margaret as we traveled with them for ministry, and we know that they truly live their lives each day relying on the One who can carry them through the challenges of life. They continue to model the seemingly simple act of total dependence on God. God has used them to bless our ministry, our family, and our lives personally. Their amazing example of faithfulness in their ministry and marriage has had a profound impact on us. We have laughed and cried together, and our lives are richer because of their writing, ministry, and friendship. It is our pleasure to introduce this book, which recounts the work of God in Margaret and Paul's lives. He has used their story to touch the hearts and lives of people of every age and across many different cultures.

CATHY SMITH
DAVID SMITH,
President and CEO of ABWE (Across Borders for World Evangelism) Canada, a sending mission agency based in London, Ontario

Footprints in the Sand

Margaret Fishback Powers

One night I dreamed a dream.
I was walking along the beach with my Lord.
Across the dark sky flashed scenes from my life.
For each scene, I noticed two sets
of footprints in the sand,
one belonging to me
and one to my Lord.
When the last scene of my life shot before me
I looked back at the footprints in the sand.
There was only one set of footprints.
I realized that this was at the lowest
and saddest times of my life.
This always bothered me
and I questioned the Lord
about my dilemma.
"Lord, You told me when I decided to follow You,
You would walk and talk with me all the way.
But I'm aware that during the most troublesome

times of my life there is only one set of footprints.
I just don't understand why, when I needed You
  most,
You leave me."
He whispered, "My precious child,
I love you and will never leave you,
never, ever, during your trials and testings.
When you saw only one set of footprints
it was then that I carried you."

Introduction

"Footprints in the Sand" has touched people around the world during their happy moments and during their times of fear, loneliness, sadness, and desperation.

My own missionary, Dr. Helen Roseveare (my mother's prayer partner), was a medical missionary in Zaire. In the 1960s, she was caught up in the war there. My handwritten "Footprints" poem was in her pocket. It was just after I had penned it, in the fall of 1964. My mother shared a copy with her. God miraculously preserved her life, against all odds. I'm certain there are many stories still to be written and shared with us about how the poem has blessed and comforted individuals.

I believe "Footprints" has such a universal appeal because it has a visual effect. People can grasp the image—we see it in our mind's eye. It is a moving image to which people of all ages can relate: a walk on the beach . . . memories of the beach, with reflections on childhood . . . playing in the sandbox at the beach on a hot day . . .

But I never would have dreamed that this appeal would be so universal. I'm still amazed today, and I'm sure my family is as well.

It is very important, however, that the message of my life's values be passed on to others, particularly to those who need it during their dark hours, so that it may provide encouragement and support during their pressing decisions. The message is personal and imprinted on each person differently, to suit one's own needs. That is why everyone has an individual story to tell. We are like snowflakes—unique.

The poem or books do not reach people only in times of difficulty but in every aspect of life here on Earth. I remember meeting with a taxi-driver friend in London. His rabbi friend in Tel Aviv had read "Footprints" during a wedding ceremony in Jerusalem. The rabbi wanted to provide encouragement to the new couple while gently pointing out how they might cope if there were difficulties down the road. Our friend loved my books, and it was an honor to sign cards and books for him to send to his family and friends in both Israel and London.

Each reader interprets the poem's message—written and visual—to answer his or her own heart's needs. In England and on islands in the Caribbean, children draw or paint pictures to illustrate the "Footprints" poem. It is amazing to see the variety of visual images they produce.

***

Since the initial release of *Footprints: The True Story Behind the Poem That Inspired Millions*, thousands of cards have been forwarded to me from my publisher's offices worldwide—letters that express a wide range of thoughts and emotions. Those who wrote had been touched by the poem, by the book, or by one of the many personal speaking engagements I have made around the world with my missionary evangelist husband, Paul.

I received so many wonderful letters, in fact, that some of them were compiled in a book called *Friends of Footprints*. I have included a sampling of letters, including ones received very recently, for your reading pleasure and inspiration. I am also pleased to share a selection of my other poems, including ones that are mentioned in the pages of this book. In this special new edition, I also reflect on some of the events that I share in this book. Each chapter ends with an informal "interview" question. In my response, I try to provide some of my thoughts, impressions, and feelings about these important moments in my life.

Part One—Comfort

The righteous cry out, and the Lord hears them;
he delivers them from all their troubles.

—Psalm 34:17

Chapter 1

I Know the Author

But those who hope in the Lord
will renew their strength.
They will soar on wings like eagles;
they will run and not grow weary,
they will walk and not be faint.

—Isaiah 40:31

"Oh, it's always so good to be home." I sighed as I said this, looking at Paul, my husband, who was stretched out, relaxing. We'd been woken up early by the birds outside our window.

"Make the most of it, Margie," he responded, "we'll be off again tomorrow."

"Where to this time?" I asked, weariness sounding in my voice.

"Vancouver."

We'd just returned from a two-month series of church camps in Washington State. Summer was always our busiest season. Our Little People's Ministry, which was dedicated to evangelism—to equipping and encouraging children to learn and grow spiritually—found us hopping from one camp, church, and crusade to another. Not that it wasn't challenging and fulfilling—of course it was; in fact, it was one of the dreams of our lives come true—but toward the middle of the summer we were more than ready to kick back and relax at our home in Coquitlam, British Columbia.

Now it was August. As I looked at our travel itinerary, observing the date—Monday, August 7, 1989, a Canadian holiday—I thought we would at least sleep in. I didn't know it at the time, but the date was to be forever imprinted in our memories—an unforgettable day with triple events that would be seared in our minds for life.

It was still very early that Monday morning when the phone rang. "I'll get it; stay put," I said to my husband.

"Hi, Mom, how's everything?"

"It's Paula." I mouthed the words to Paul. "Everything's fine," I assured our daughter, "but we were just saying how good it felt to be home."

"Well, in that case, maybe I shouldn't ask you this," she said, then hesitated. It was only a momentary pause. "How would you like to drive a carload of kids up to Golden Ears and picnic at the Lower Falls?" Paula knew what pushovers we were for kids. Golden Ears was a vast provincial park about ten miles away. "I need an extra vehicle—someone dropped out." She paused briefly again. "If you'll do it, the sooner you can come and meet us at the church, the better. Everyone's waiting. They're anxious to get this show on the road."

I glanced at Paul. "Okay, we'll come," I promised. I already knew what Paul's reaction would be. There just wasn't anything he wouldn't do for kids, his own childhood had been so traumatic.

"Thanks, Mom, I knew I could count on you and Dad. Bring your swimsuit and wear your shorts."

I quickly pulled on my swimsuit, slipped on a pair of shorts over it, and reached for the top and shirt jacket I'd worn the day before. "I'll leave all this stuff where it is," I said, remembering everything in the pockets.

9

"Yes, don't take time to clean out your pockets," Paul said. A few minutes later we were on our way out the door. As we drove the short distance to the church where Paula and the kids were waiting, I felt in the pockets of the shirt jacket, fingering the bottle of Paul's heart pills and another bottle of extra-strength Tylenol. *Why do I always load myself down with this stuff?* I asked myself.

We did a quick drive-through at McDonald's on our way out of town, the back of the van filled with kids. "Golden Ears Park, here we come!" one of the kids shouted, and we all laughed. It was going to be a fun day. We enjoyed being with Paula and her young charges. We often jokingly said to each other and our friends that our daughters, Tina and Paula, and their young friends kept us on our toes. There's no time to think about advancing years when you're around young people.

"What a gorgeous day," I said. Everyone agreed that they'd picked the right day. Twice before, the outing had been canceled because of inclement weather—British Columbia's liquid sunshine.

Upon arrival at the park, we joined the others clambering out of cars. A few instructions to the

group from Paula about the need to be careful—
the rocks would be slippery and we'd be crossing
the top of Lower Falls on a rock ledge—and we all
took off. Just before leaving, Paula explained, "Now
listen, you guys, there's a forty-foot-deep glacier
pool off one side. No funny stuff, okay?"

We were proud of our beautiful daughter. She
had such a love for young people, and she and
her sister had always been a part of our work with
youth. They were extremely gifted ventriloquists,
and it was a delight to be around them. Now, I
watched Paula lead the kids, her long strawberry-
blonde hair swinging free as we approached the
rock ledge walkway.

We all made our way cautiously across the slippery rocks and then found perches for ourselves
as we paused to rest and enjoy the breathtakingly
beautiful scenery. We watched rather anxiously as
some older fellows (not part of our group) dove
into the glacier pool from high atop a rock perch.
"That water is ice-cold," I called to Paula. "How
can they stand it?"

"I don't know," she called back, shaking her head,
"I'm glad it's not me!"

Paul elected to stay on the other side of the glacier pool, where there was another, smaller pocket of water that looked inviting. He had said to me, "This is where I'm going to read." I knew he wanted to prepare for the Vancouver meetings. He carefully made his way around to where he could enjoy the beauty and have some seclusion.

We saw lots of swimmers and sunbathers enjoying themselves on the rocks and in the water. Looking down, we could see others amusing themselves at the base of the falls and in the river. I couldn't help thinking that there should be barricades or fences, and signs warning people that it was dangerous and slippery in places.

"It's so beautiful up here," one of the girls remarked.

"Absolutely heavenly," I replied, thinking to myself that it felt as if we were so close to heaven that we could almost reach up and touch God. Spruce and pine trees towered above us, the sun filtering through. The glacier water was emerald-green.

After sunning a while, I looked at my watch and called across to my husband, "Paul, it's 2:15." Paul glanced up from his reading and acknowledged that he'd heard me.

Just then, Paula said, "I'm going back across to where Dad is." She started out over the rock ledge. At the same time, somewhere nearby, a dog barked, startling me.

As a mother, I thought about the sixty-eight-foot falls on the one side and the forty-foot-deep glacier pool on the other, and called out, cautioning Paula, "Oh, be careful!" I watched as she inched her way along. Paul was also watching as she made her way. He stood up and held out his hand to reach for her when she got closer. At that moment she missed her footing and fell into a whirlpool of water. It sucked her into its vortex, spinning her around three times, and before any of us knew what was happening, she was spun out and over the falls.

Everyone was screaming. I jumped to my feet, screaming too. I couldn't help Paula. What should I do? I glanced across at my husband and saw him clutch his chest and fall. At that moment, I knew he was having a heart attack—I could actually see his color change. It was all happening as if in slow motion, but the confusion was terrible, and I feared for the lives of the other young people if they should panic. I turned my back momentarily to face the kids, who were hysterical. "We must pray," I shouted, crying out, "O God, help us!"

I reached around my neck for a necklace that Paul had given me on our twenty-third wedding anniversary just the year before. I glanced down at the eagle mounted on black onyx and sent a tele-gram-prayer heavenward: "Lord, if You are going to take Paula, take her without too much pain, and O God, spare my husband."

I thought my daughter must surely be dead. How could anyone survive a sixty-eight-foot fall into glacier-cold water? I knew I had to get to my husband, but I instinctively also knew I couldn't trust my shaky legs to the slippery rock ledge. Just as I was about to enter the water to swim across, a man called to me from where my husband was. "I'm going to throw this rope across the pool. My son is alongside you; he'll grab it. Hang on to the rope as you swim across."

What I didn't know was that the man's wife was a nurse who was at that very moment administering aid to Paul. Earlier that day, as they left home, the man had grabbed the rope that they used to tether their dog, and his son had said to him, "What are you doing with that rope?" "I don't know," he'd replied as he stuck it in his pocket. Now I was holding on to the rope with one hand as I swam with the other. The water was icy cold, but I was oblivious to the temperature as I made my way across.

Down below, some boys on the rocks at the base of the falls saw a body floating by and, thinking it was a corpse, pulled it ashore. A woman sunning on the rocks observed all this, rushed over, and immediately began resuscitation. I found out later that this woman was a nurse trained specifically in drowning accidents.

I struggled onto the rocks, anxious to reach my husband's side, the man who had been holding the rope helping me. But somehow, in my desperate and frantic attempt, I slipped several times on the slimy rocks and broke my right arm. It hung limp at my side, and as soon as I was out of the water, I was aware of excruciating pain. Then I saw a woman bending over Paul. The man told me, "She's a nurse, trained in cardiac arrest."

"Thank God," I murmured, my whole body

shaking uncontrollably. Suddenly I remembered Paul's heart medicine and told the nurse that in my left pocket was a bottle of Nitrol. Someone noticed me trembling and thoughtfully threw a large towel around me.

At one point, the nurse turned and calmly said, "They tell me that's your daughter who went over the falls. My sister-in-law is down below; she's a nurse trained in water rescue."

I fell back on the rocks, overcome with emotion, grateful to think that perhaps Paula had been rescued. I was just about to pass out when I heard the nurse add, "Oh, it's too bad we don't have some pain medicine." I tried reaching into my right pocket but could only motion.

"She's a walking pharmacy," the woman said as she found the bottle of extra-strength Tylenol.

The presence of both of these nurses was amazing, but they explained that they were on strike at the provincial hospitals, which was why they were at the park on an outing. One of the swimmers we'd seen diving was also a long-distance runner. He immediately took off, running to reach the nearest phone and call in ambulances for help. Somehow the kids all carefully made their way back to the cars, waiting and praying while anxiously wondering what was to be the outcome of all this.

A search-and-rescue team arrived first and was already starting to carry us out when the ambulances came. Stretchers were then brought in. Four hours after the accidents, we were in the emergency room at Maple Ridge General Hospital. At three in the morning I learned that X-rays had revealed that Paula had a broken neck, her arm had been pulled out of its socket, and she had a perforated kidney and liver. She was a gravely injured young woman, but she was alive.

Nearby, in the intensive-care ward, my husband lay hooked to heart monitors and intravenous tubes. A few hours later a nurse came and asked him, "Mr. Powers, would you like me to pray for you, your daughter, and your wife?" He nodded yes, and so she prayed.

When she finished praying, she said, "I think it would help you if I read a little piece I have here in my pocket," and she pulled out a card. Holding my husband's hand, she quietly read:

One night I dreamed a dream.
I was walking along the beach with my Lord.
Across the dark sky flashed scenes from my life.
For each scene, I noticed two sets
of footprints in the sand,
one belonging to me
and one to my Lord.
When the last scene of my life shot before me
I looked back at the footprints in the sand.
There was only one set of footprints.
I realized that this was at the lowest
and saddest times of my life.
This always bothered me
and I questioned the Lord
about my dilemma.
"Lord, You told me when I decided to follow You,
You would walk and talk with me all the way.
But I'm aware that during the most troublesome
times of my life there is only one set of footprints.
I just don't understand why, when I needed You
    most,
You leave me."
He whispered, "My precious child,
I love you and will never leave you,

never, ever, during your trials and testings.
When you saw only one set of footprints
it was then that I carried you."

When the nurse finished reading, she looked at my husband and said, "I don't know the author; it's anonymous."

Paul lifted his hand very weakly and said, "I do. I know the author." The nurse thought he wasn't fully conscious because of the medication he'd been given, but Paul said again, "I know the author very well . . . she's my wife."

***

Reflections on Chapter 1

You shared Paul's words as he lay in intensive care having suffered a major heart attack. At the same time, your daughter Paula was gravely injured. Paul's nurse quietly read "Footprints" to comfort him, thinking it was by an anonymous poet. When she finished, Paul said to her, "I know the author very well . . . she's my wife." No doubt you have continued to reflect on those events and on Paul's words. Would you like to share some of your thoughts?

On August 7, 1989, at 2:15 in the afternoon, our family suffered great trauma when our youngest daughter was swept over a waterfall in front of our eyes. She has survived and is thriving. As we have reflected on this major event in our lives, we realized that God was speaking to us again and reminding us that He would never leave us or forsake us. He is there all the time while we are going through the difficulties, and He will help us carry on. Many times over the years of ministry, that single event has come back to our minds to encourage us. The verse that appears in various books throughout the Scripture is Hebrews 13:5, "Never will I leave you; never will I forsake you," and it is just as important to me today.

Part Two—Prelude

Finally, all of you, live in harmony with one another; be sympathetic, love as brothers, be compassionate and humble.

—*1 Peter 3:8*

Chapter 2

ENCOUNTER WITH DESTINY

Across the dark sky flashed scenes from my life.

With my husband and daughter in hospital beds, both in intensive care, and with my arm in a cast, the landscape of our lives seemed overshadowed by a dark sky. Yet Paul and Paula were alive, miraculously so, and I knew from past experience that during this troublesome time we would be carried. God had carried us before; He would carry us now.

Paul told me about the nurse reading the "Footprints" poem. We were both overwhelmed to think that something I'd written in 1964 was now speaking so much comfort to our hearts more than twenty years later. My mind reached back to embrace treasured memories as I reflected on our lives.

I remembered my first two meetings with Paul Powers. The second time, his jeans were dirty—in fact, his clothes were cobwebby. Not exactly a picture of the well-groomed, dignified, irresistible Prince Charming every girl dreams of riding off with into the future! I was living in the High Park area of Toronto, and my younger brother, Jim, had asked me to accompany him and our sister Ruby to a bookstore. While we were there, we bumped into Paul, who was working in the store. "Hey, great to see you," Paul and Jim both exclaimed as they slapped each other on the shoulder.

"Oh, these are my sisters Margie and Ruby," Jim added, offhandedly introducing us. "I think you may have met once, three or four years ago, out at the farm. Girls, this is Paul Powers. We were buddies in high school."

I couldn't tell if Paul remembered me from that first meeting, but I remembered him. In fact, I remembered that occasion distinctly, because he was in and out quite fast that day and I'd said to my mother, "That's one guy I wouldn't marry if he was the last man on Earth!"

I wouldn't have admitted it at the time, but I was

probably miffed because he didn't pay more attention to me. My mother came to his defense. "He's delivering a film for our high-school Bible club, and he doesn't have time to spare. He just wanted to say a quick hello to Jim. He's on his way to a Youth for Christ rally in Simcoe." I remembered that Jim had said Paul was attending the London (Ontario) College of Bible and Missions.

Now we were face to face again and I was sizing him up. He was about twenty-five—four years older than I was. I couldn't help but notice that behind his dark-rimmed glasses, his blue-gray eyes fairly danced. In spite of his grubby appearance, he was good-looking, with his dark hair and suntanned face.

He apologized for his dirty clothes. "I'm moving things around," he said, wiping his perspiring face. It was a hot August afternoon, and I was suddenly conscious of my own appearance, wondering how I looked. His gaze was so penetrating. He had a book in his hands and he extended it to me.

He said, "Are you married?"

I looked at the title and read *How to Have a Happy Marriage*. His question caught me by surprise, as he no doubt knew it would. Did I detect a smile on his face? The question made me upset, and I quickly retorted, "No, and I don't plan to get married, either!" I was really short with him. Today he would tell you that I "barbed" at him and that I "clipped" him, intending to put him in his place. I softened my response somewhat, however, by asking him, "Are you married?"

He grinned and replied, "No, but I'm sure thinking about it."

What Paul didn't know was that I was still getting over a broken relationship, and I wasn't thinking too kindly about any man at that point.

"You know, I think we all need a cool drink," Paul said. "Let's go downstairs to the Honeydew Restaurant." I was a bit reluctant, but Ruby and Jim thought it was a great idea. "Their specialty is this fantastic honeydew drink—honey, orange juice, milk, and some honeydew melon juice," Paul explained.

The drink was refreshing. Paul was a delightful conversationalist and had us all laughing.

"What brings you to Toronto?" Paul asked me.

"I'm taking some summer-school classes in connection with my work as a teacher," I replied. I'd been teaching for three years; Ruby was still in high school. "And I'm helping Jim with his work." I didn't tell him then what Jim's work was.

"By the way, Paul," Jim said, "we're going to the Ex on Saturday." The Ex, the Canadian National Exhibition, was an annual treat for us, with its displays and contests and exciting atmosphere. "Have you been yet?"

"No," he replied, "but I'd like to go. I can get Saturday off. Margie, mind if I come along? I'd like to take you."

A date? I fumbled for an excuse. There was something sweet about this fellow, even if he was a tad earnest. You need some fun, I rationalized to myself. But that would be it. Just some time out for fun. "You'll never regret saying yes," Paul promised, the excitement in his eyes nearly convincing me that it was time.

That's how it happened that I spent the following Saturday with this fellow whose conversation was so refreshing. After Paul finally showed up to meet us at the funeral parlor where my brother worked and stayed, we were on our way in Jim's car. "You didn't tell me you lived in a mortuary,"

Paul quipped. "It took me a while to find this place." The way he said it, it became a big joke. At first, though, I thought he'd changed his mind about coming with us.

It had rained earlier, and the drenching downpour had turned the Exhibition parking lot into a bog. Paul got out of the car, sloshed over to my open door, and saw me hesitate, my feet dangling over a muddy puddle. In an instant, he reached inside the car, saying, "Here, let me lift you out" as he swept me up in his strong arms, depositing me safely beyond the puddle.

As we walked along, I slipped and almost fell. Paul grabbed my arm. "You're so tiny," he said, "I'm going to have to carry you or we'll lose you in one of these puddles!" We laughed. But I didn't think it was so funny when we reached the turnstiles and the gatekeeper charged him for one adult and one child. It didn't help when Paul corrected the man and he looked flustered and said, "Oh, I thought she was your daughter." I'd been mistaken for a child before, being under five feet tall, so I took it as a good sport, but I suddenly knew I didn't want to be mistaken for Paul Powers' daughter.

The wide-striped exposition tents billowed in the wind, and the Ferris wheel and the many other rides packed with merry-makers jostling one another added to the carnival atmosphere. The music all but drowned out our conversation.

Neither of us really cared for the rides, but we tried a few. We enjoyed the home shows and displays more than anything, and there we could hear each other. We quickly found ourselves talking about every subject imaginable—the things we enjoyed, such as music, good books, and other mutual interests.

At one point we found a more secluded place to rest and Paul asked about my work as a missionary teacher in Maniwaki, Quebec, and the multilingual children I'd been teaching in the first three grades of school. "Illness forced me to give that up," I explained. "It broke my heart. But I'll be teaching near Tillsonburg this fall."

Paul was very kind as he expressed concern. "May I ask what happened?"

"There was an electrical storm," I said slowly, remembering with pain the events of May 1963. "Lightning flashed from mountain peak to mountain peak, alarming some of the students, but most were accustomed to the daytime storms. I had always cautioned my pupils to keep the windows closed during storms like that. However, Jimmie, one of the students, opened the window 'only a wee crack,' as he said, to get a breath of fresh air. Poor Jimmie suffered from cerebral palsy."

I looked into Paul's face. He showed such interest that I continued. "A bolt of lightning flashed through the open window as I stood at the blackboard writing lessons, and sparks flew from the ends of my fingers. I was thrown down and came to my senses on the floor against the wall of the classroom. Weakly, I picked myself up, dusted myself off, and reassured the children as best I could, then went back to the lessons.

"But the electrical shock made me very dizzy and ill. As the day progressed, the milk chart and attendance sheet jumped up and down before my bleary eyes. That afternoon I dismissed the class early and cradled my head in my arms on the desk. The pain was almost unbearable. In the days that followed, I became increasingly ill, and the pain in my back and arm increased to the point where I was visibly shaking most of the time.

"Still, I worked that next week. But on Friday, when my best friend, Betty Reside, came to visit, she took one look at me and rushed me off to the hospital, where I remained for some time. My condition was much more serious than any of us had originally thought, and it was weeks before I was able to go home. The school-board officers were unable to renew my teaching contract, as I had no guarantee of complete recovery. That's when I came back home."

Paul had been very quiet through my lengthy explanation, but his grip on my hands was tender yet strong, and this imparted strength to me. I felt so comfortable in his presence as his eyes searched mine. "God has been my strength, Paul," I confided, "and He has been carrying me through."

When we started talking about the Lord, we knew we were on the same wavelength. The more we shared events from our lives, the more comfortable we felt with each other. We discovered that we had a mutual desire to reach people and to impact their lives with the truths of God's Word. An initial bonding took place that had its roots in our desire to have our steps ordered by the Lord.

Paul would tell you that by the end of the day

he was smitten, that he was head over heels in love with me, and that I had "the right bait."

We had fun that Saturday at the Exhibition. Paul says that my "cat eyes" were sparkling by the end of the day, that he could tell I enjoyed life and having fun, but that there were some other hurts and bad experiences I hadn't shared with him that needed to be put behind me. He determined in his heart that he would help me to forget. I didn't know that he also had a past that he was seeking to forget, with God's help—that in fact, he was a victim of child abuse. There was much we needed to learn about each other, and we would in the days ahead. I felt inexplicably drawn to him.

My brother, sister, and I had accepted a dinner invitation for that evening, and we asked Paul to come along. It was the perfect climax to a wonderful day. Good fun and the beginning of a relationship that would go through lots of troublesome times. But we would have each other. More important, the two of us had the Lord walking with us.

That memorable Saturday evening, Jim offered to give Paul a lift back to his apartment. He and I sat together in the back seat, still talking. Just as

Jim pulled up to Paul's door, he said, "Good night," and kissed me.

It surprised me, but not unpleasantly. "I had a really great time," I told him.

"Me too," he said. "How about if I write you?"

As we drove away, I told my brother, "He had a nice day, but he won't write." How wrong I was!

***

Reflections on Chapter 2

As you reflect on your second meeting with Paul, you describe him as "not exactly a picture of the well-groomed, dignified, irresistible Prince Charming every girl dreams of riding off with into the future." But after spending a day together, you admit that your first impressions proved quite wrong. Paul determined that he would help you forget the hurts in your life, and you understood that there was much you needed to learn about each other. I imagine we've all jumped to incorrect conclusions. What can we learn from mistaken first impressions?

The life lesson I derived from this encounter was that first impressions and quick decisions or evaluations can sometimes be misguided by preconceived expectations. It is very important to get to know each other patiently, and not to plan in our minds changes that we may think need to be made.

Chapter 3

FALTERING STEPS

*My precious child, I love you and will never
leave you.*

Sometimes nature gets angry in a very random
and violent way. At any given moment around
the world, there are more than a thousand storms,
and oftentimes those storms give birth to lightning.
And lightning can kill.

Scientists have found that one stroke of lightning
produces more than 15 million volts of electricity.
A charge between a cloud and the Earth may measure as much as eight miles long, traveling at a rate
of 100 million feet per second. Lightning reaching between oppositely charged clouds may have a
length of twenty miles.

Although I was a schoolteacher, I couldn't have told you these things; nor could I have told you that lightning kills more people (on average) per year than hurricanes and tornadoes combined. I didn't know that lightning blasts through the atmosphere at an estimated rate of two billion flashes a year. Lightning kills one person and injures four others every day in the United States alone. Yet the chances of being struck by lightning are about one in a million. The chances of being struck and surviving are even more remote. As one news reporter wrote: "The chance of surviving a lightning strike is a roll of the dice."

I survived, but one of my students didn't. A great sadness invaded my young life that day I was struck by a flash of lightning as I stood before my class.

His name was Alfred. He was just a tiny boy, but he made a big impact on my life. Alfred introduced me to death in a way that I'd never been touched by it before.

Alfred had hardly spoken a word for the entire year, and now here it was May; the school year was almost over. I'd had the children make beautiful hexagonal baskets, and most of them had taken their baskets home at least a month before. When

I asked Alfred why he delayed, he gently whispered that he was waiting for the right and special moment when his basket could be filled.

That afternoon, as I was feeling the effects of the electrical jolt, Alfred stood beside me, an angelic smile breaking over his face. "See this, Teacher," he said, holding up the largest mass of yellow dandelions I had ever seen.

They were so healthy and pretty, I hated to cut the stems off to make them fit in his little basket, but that's what he was asking me to do. He carefully placed the flowers in his pretty basket and then raced out the door to the waiting bus. I could still see him waving happily as he boarded.

At that point, I collapsed onto one of the student desks and thanked the Lord that some progress had been made with wee Alfred. He really could talk after all!

Shortly after that, I left for my boarding house. I rested for a couple of hours, but the pain in my right arm had been steadily increasing since the shock of a few hours before. The electrical storm was now at its finest and fullest. I was glad to be inside where it was cozy, safe, and warm.

As I sat propped up in bed, trying to catch up on my French studies, I found it difficult to concentrate. Then the phone rang. I couldn't believe what I was hearing. My mind refused to comprehend it. "No, no, it can't be," I said, at the same time fighting the nausea that suddenly gripped me. But it was true.

My caller informed me that wee Alfred had been pushing his little sisters into the house when a bolt of lightning had struck him down. Although barely conscious, he had insisted that his parents allow him to take along his little basket when they drove him to the hospital. He had died shortly after his arrival there.

The days that followed were extremely trying for me. It was with much difficulty that I assumed the teacher's role—attending the memorial service for this darling child and playing the organ. In the days that followed, I often found myself engulfed in tears. Why Alfred? Why him? Why wasn't it me? My mind replayed the last few moments I'd had with my student. He had been such a sweet and gentle little boy.

I began to think about death. Solemn thoughts

for a young woman. I turned the pages of my Bible, seeking help. It would become a habit of the heart—looking into God's Word for direction and for answers to my questions. I was not disappointed. In Jeremiah 10:23 I found God speaking to an ancient prophet, telling him that our lives are not our own; that it is not for us to direct our steps.

It made me think. We want heaven populated with the elderly, not children or young people in what we feel is their prime of life. But Jesus loved the children when He was here on Earth. He gathered them about Him, and told us to be like them. Of course, He would want them in heaven also. I remembered Alfred's trusting ways, his quietness and kindness.

I found other verses in the Bible that assured me that death is not the end, that for those who love God and are His children through believing in His Son, Jesus, and accepting Him into their lives, eternal life in heaven is assured. Heaven is a prepared place for a prepared people.

I remembered Jesus' words to His disciples concerning heaven: "Do not let your hearts be troubled. Trust in God; trust also in me. In my Father's house are many rooms; if it were not so, I would have told you. I am going there to prepare a place for you" (John 14:1–2).

As I shared with my students my understanding of death and heaven, I discovered that they were accepting death in a beautiful, childlike, and peaceful manner. They were very subdued, and I think they missed their usually silent friend's presence. One wee girl assured me that death was like being carried home to heaven in Jesus' arms, where He would put us gently down to sleep on His big white pillow. Such an imagination! And such trust! She encouraged me, her teacher, never to be afraid, as God was always there. Her words were like an echo in the back of my mind as one day I wrote, "My precious child, I love you and will never leave you . . ."

My students gave me much-needed comfort and strength throughout the next few days. I would need it even more in the days ahead. I wasn't able to finish the rest of the school year, for a few days after that I was taken to the hospital, and the physical effects of the electrical jolt were such that it took a few months before I began to recover. I had to give up my class and move home with my parents. I suffered extreme migraine headaches as a result of the shock, and during treatment my long, curly auburn hair fell out. As it grew back, I was left with one giant patch of white that would remain with me throughout my life, a reminder always to be thankful for each day that God gives.

Recovering from the emotional effects took somewhat longer. During that period of my life, I discovered that some people cannot understand or accept death or illness. They search in the wrong places for answers to their questions. They become angry with God.

Although I didn't fully understand it at the time, in God's good providence, a relationship I thought was headed somewhere was terminated. If I had fought to hold onto the relationship, if I had made compromises, things might have turned out differently. But I could not give up my beliefs.

At the time, I felt it to be a very sad period of my life. Certainly I overdramatized it in my mind—the poet in me was always seeking ways to express herself, and I was still quite young. I had some maturing to do, and heartaches are a part of the learning and growing process. Friends called me a hopeless romantic; now I felt only hopeless.

Slowly, however, while recuperating at our family farmhouse in Tillsonburg, I began to recognize that I needed to trust God fully with the events that came into my life.

Today I can confidently say that I know that anyone who trusts God can be sure that He is ordering not only our steps but also our stops. And even when we feel we are walking a lonely, difficult, or sad path, we are not alone. His words ring true:

> *"My precious child,*
> *I love you and will never leave you,*
> *never, ever, during your trials and testings.*
> *When you saw only one set of footprints*
> *it was then that I carried you."*

***

Reflections on Chapter 3

In the tribute to your sweet young student Alfred, you write that heartaches are part of the learning and growing process. And that even when we feel we are walking a lonely, difficult, or sad path, we are not alone. This, of course, is the very theme of "Footprints." Am I correct in understanding that, in the time leading up to the creation of the poem, you were searching for direction?

Yes, that is correct. I was still recovering from the loss of my young student, while the dream of continuing my teaching career seemed to be fading because of my serious illness. There were also a few personal elements with which I was struggling at the time. Fortunately, I have always developed long-lasting friendships. Among my dearest friends I count people I met during those days of "trials and testings." And I am blessed to have new friends in my life as well.

Chapter 4

Love Letters Straight
from the Heart

As for God, his way is perfect.

—Psalm 18:30

The joy-filled Saturday with Paul Powers at the Canadian National Exhibition prompted a flood of thoughts in the days following. I reflected on the events that had taken place since May and found, to my surprise and delight, that my perspective had changed considerably just since the encounter with Paul.

I even anticipated the daily trip to the mailbox and was rewarded when, midway through the week, there was a letter from Toronto bearing Paul's return address. He had written to me the very next day, and now I held his letter in my hands. To say I was pleased and excited would be an understatement. Eagerly I found a quiet place where I would be undisturbed and started reading.

Paul wrote another letter on Wednesday, which I received on Friday. His letters began to reveal things about him that I had only surmised—I had sensed his spiritual depth, but because our time together had been so short, I hadn't been quite able to fully grasp or appreciate it.

I was headed for the mailbox to send Paul a letter on Saturday when he showed up in person with my brother. Jim had invited him to the farm for the weekend but hadn't called to let us know. I handed Paul my letter, and once again he came up with one of his quips: "Personal delivery, no less!"

"It's great that you're here," I remember saying, trying to not sound too excited.

Paul immediately offered his services to my father, and Dad took him up on it. Paul cut the lawn—a half-acre—with our old push mower and helped my father get rid of a hornet's nest under the eaves. I was out there pulling weeds, hoeing in the garden, raking up the grass—just so I could be near Paul, although I wouldn't have admitted it to anyone, not even to myself.

In the evening, we played Monopoly and popped corn. We had a wonderful time, and we all got to know Paul better.

On Sunday we attended our church, the North Broadway Baptist Church, where Paul was reunited with a London Bible College friend, our pastor, Lambert Baptist. The rest of the day flew by all too fast, and before we knew it, Jim and Paul were headed back to Toronto. Paul promised to write some more and, busy as he was, he kept his word by writing two or three times weekly for the next several weeks. I wrote him lots of letters, too. Once I mailed three in a single day! I was revealing more about myself to him than I'd ever imagined wanting to. I told him things about myself I'd never told anyone. We really were becoming friends, close friends. And whenever he could, he'd come to the farm to visit.

"Tell me about your childhood," he said on one of those visits. "Have you always loved the piano?"

"You should ask my parents about that," I responded. "Oh, Paul, you won't believe it, but I actually composed music in my sleep. I was a sleep-walker when I was little, and in the middle of the night I'd get up, come downstairs, and sit at the piano. The rest of the family didn't much appreciate it." We laughed.

"But in answer to your question, my parents sacrificed to get a piano for me. I started playing by ear at age six. My father used to turn on the radio, hear a song he liked, and say, 'Now, Midge, hear that? I'll turn the radio off, and you play it on the piano,' and that's what I'd do. I wanted lessons, and people used to tell me that now I would never be able to learn from lessons. But I made up my mind that I'd prove them wrong. So, at age thirteen, I started learning properly."

"And today you're studying to be a composer and concert pianist," Paul said admiringly. "God has really gifted you, Marge."

I thanked him for his compliments and told him that I appreciated his understanding that gifted-ness—whatever form it takes—is from God. "I want my poetry and music to always be an expression of what God has put into my heart and soul," I said, and I really meant it.

"They will, Margie," he said quietly, patting my hands, "they will." There were tears in his eyes.

"Tell me about your childhood, Paul," I said.

He hesitated and then answered. "It bears no resemblance to your happy and carefree childhood, Margie . . ."

It was then that I began to learn about Paul's past. I discovered things that, in the privacy of my own room as I reflected on what he had told me, made me sob. I wept in Paul's presence, too; there was no way I could keep back the tears.

His mother had died when he was still very young, and what followed can only be described as child abuse. As Dr. James Dobson said a few years ago, after interviewing Paul on his Focus on the Family radio program, "Paul Powers was one of the most pathetic victims of child abuse I have ever known."

Immediately following the death of his mother, as this terrified seven-year-old stood by, sobbing his little heart out, his drunken father struck him in the face with his fist, knocking him all the way across the room. But the beating didn't stop there. With blood streaming from Paul's nose and mouth, his father kicked and stomped on him, shouting,

"For cryin' out loud! Shut up, you stupid kid! Real men don't cry; babies cry." He continued kicking him in the side, the face, everywhere.

The same ambulance that carried Paul's dead mother away also carried Paul to the hospital, where he spent several days being treated for a broken wrist, broken ribs, a badly swollen eye, lacerations, and several missing teeth. "But I didn't cry," Paul told me. "I vowed I'd never cry again."

Paul lost not only his mother that day but also his childhood. He became a bitter little boy forced to be a "man" overnight, and in the process, he paid a terrible price. He had a tragic childhood marred by the heavy drinking of his father, who was often in a drunken stupor, and then his father's remarriage, with more children being brought into the home by his stepmother, and yet more children being born in subsequent years. By the time he was eight, he had been in and out of trouble with the police, as innocent child's play with neighborhood children turned into shoplifting, gang robbery, and eventually murder.

He spent years being bounced from one reform school to another and finally did hard time in a prison that had formerly been a prisoner-of-war camp for captured German soldiers. By the time he was sixteen, he was a hardened delinquent and was taken to an even more secure prison in Guelph, Ontario, where he spent much of his time in solitary confinement. But it was there that he was given the chance to participate in a trade school, which revealed his creative abilities. This eventually resulted in privileges being granted. He was transferred to Bowmanville, where he worked in a shoe factory. The job was a turning point. While he was on the work-release program, he boarded with an elderly Christian couple, Clara and Clarence Adams, and his life changed dramatically.

"I was invited to a Youth for Christ meeting by a girl I'd been dating," he explained to me, "and I went—several times, in fact." His voice broke as he talked to me, and tears came into his eyes.

"You're crying," I said gently.

"Yes," he said, "I'd spent all those years locking things up since my mother died, and the dam finally burst following one of those meetings. God and I had a good talk. I sought Jesus' forgiveness, like the thief on the cross, whom I'd heard about the night before. God the Father whispered that He loved me, and I believed Him. Now I can cry and know it's okay . . ."

In September 1959 he had moved to London, Ontario, to do Youth for Christ work in juvenile and family court, as well as in area rallies. He was now doing area rallies around Belleville, as well as counseling young offenders—youths going through much of the turmoil he himself had suffered.

Whatever Paul didn't tell me that day soon found its way into his letters, as our weekly correspondence continued. Before long I knew these were love letters straight from his heart, and the words "I love you" began to surface.

***

Reflections on Chapter 4

This was a difficult, yet ultimately an uplifting, chapter to read. You write about your carefree youth and compare it with Paul's horrific childhood. This is a chapter about forgiveness, the strength to turn one's life around, and our ability to use the lessons from our life so we may help others. What is the most important message we can take from these pages?

According to the Bible, we read many Scriptures that say God does not give up on His children. It is a lesson to learn that we should not give up, either. Remember, the Scripture says, "They who have been forgiven much, must therefore liberally forgive." It doesn't mean it is easy. But over time, and with maturity, we are able to apply this potent life lesson.

Part Three—Reflection

That you may live a life worthy of the Lord and may please him in every way: bearing fruit in every good work.

—*Colossians 1:10*

Chapter 5

WHAT IS GOD SAYING?

Live as children of light . . .
and find out what pleases the Lord.
—*Ephesians 5:8–10*

The conversations and correspondence with Paul made me do a lot of reflecting. As I thought about what had so dramatically shaped his life, making him into the man I knew and respected, I realized that it was time for me to reflect on my own life and where I was headed.

I had been blessed in being raised in a happy, secure home environment. I was the third in a family of six children, and our parents also cared for a foster brother, Gordon. "Three sons and three daughters," my father loved to say proudly.

"You were named after Princess Margaret Rose," he often reminded me. "Margaret Rose Fishback, that's what we decided to call you." My mother's background was Scottish; my father's parents had immigrated to Canada from Düsseldorf, Germany, before he was born. "There's a town on the border of Austria and Germany called Fishback, named for our family," he told us. He was proud of his German heritage. But one of my first recollections of anything "bad" happening to me came as a result of my German background.

It happened in the first grade. I had trouble with the teacher, not because I was slow but because I was bored. "Speak English or else," the teacher threatened. I must have picked up some German pronunciation from my father, for every time I pronounced words like free, tree, and three, and she would hit me on the knuckles with her pointer— a solid wooden stick with a black rubber tip. My knuckles were always red! I can still hear her say "Don't speak with that German sound!" and down would come the pointer. Her "or else" threats both embarrassed and scared me.

One day my father and I were sitting out on a log

having one of our heart-to-heart talks, and I told him about it. "Be proud of your ancestry," he said, adding, "Just remember what the Bible teaches, and the Ten Commandments, and don't talk back to your teacher."

It was one of my first encounters with animosity. Now, reflecting on this, I realized my teacher's hostility was due to the fact that it was World War II, and it had little or nothing to do with who I was. Later, in another class, when I wanted to do a research paper on my German background, my mother said "No!" very firmly. *Touchy-touchy*, I thought, and never brought it up again, remembering my red knuckles and the first-grade teacher.

An even earlier incident during which I felt the sting of a teacher's punishment stands out. It was in kindergarten. The teacher had a red leather strap that she used to swat us across our hands. She had gone out of the classroom and, kids being kids, we seized the opportunity—all of us, as I recall—to get up from our desks and start swinging on them in the aisles. When the teacher returned and caught us, she lined us up and had us file into the cloak-room one by one. I could hear her hit the kids ahead of me with the strap, and suddenly tears started rolling down my cheeks. I felt so bad for my classmates—worse for them than for myself. But when it was my turn, the strap hurt hardly at all. It was just a good sting. I was puzzled about that.

Did the teacher hit me less hard because I was so tiny and fragile-looking? Did she think I was a follower and quite innocent? I reflected on this, too, as I called up more memories from that time. I had cried for my classmates; I hadn't cried for myself. Crying for others is still something I do very easily; feeling Paul's pain made me weep. Crying is therapeutic. God values our tears; Psalm 56 says that He even records them. In many places we are told that God sees our tears, but we are promised that one day He will wipe away all tears from our eyes (Isaiah 25:8) and that there will be no more death or mourning or crying or pain (Revelation 21:4).

I kept my guardian angel busy, I'm quite certain. There was the day, when I was a small child, that my life was spared. My sister and I had been to Goodlett's grocery store, and on the way home a cousin started chasing me. I darted into the street, into the path of an oncoming truck, and I was hit.

The impact threw me onto the grass at the North Broadway Baptist Church. The driver stopped, picked me up, and carried me to our home just a short block away. My sister was screaming and so was I—not because I was badly hurt but because I didn't want to be carried, and probably because I feared the reprimand that would be forthcoming from my parents, who always cautioned us to look both ways before crossing the street.

There was another time, when I was about thirteen, when a big bumblebee landed on me while I was hoeing potatoes in the garden. I was very nervous about bees, since we had lost an uncle to a bee sting. I started screaming, and my brother Jim ran to rescue me. "No, no, don't touch me!" I shouted as my screams faded away, because suddenly I knew God was going to take care of me. It was like an instantaneous vision of the Lord coming down to help.

Childlike, I prayed, "Lord, take the bee away from me, and I'll let You come into my life and direct me."

You aren't supposed to bargain with God! I can almost hear someone say that. But God knew I'd been giving Him a lot of thought, and this was my moment of reckoning. You see, my older sister had become a Christian, and she kept urging me to ask Jesus into my life. I knew she prayed for me (I could hear her). I'd tell her and my mom, "I'm not interested. I want to become a concert pianist and an actress and a teacher." "She's a stubborn little thing," my mother declared more than once during those years.

I just didn't want anything to interfere with my childhood aspirations. And I certainly didn't want to change my ways or give up these dreams. What I didn't understand was that God doesn't take away—He only gives and enhances what He has already given. God is a giver. The best.

That day, after the bumblebee flew away without leaving behind its stinger, I threw down the hoe and told my mother I was going to be baptized at the church. I knew from that moment on that I would always want to show that Christ was in my life.

One other incident stood out as I reflected on my past, seeking to attach meaning to memories. I had observed how Paul's past had served as a wise teacher. He always would say, "Memories and mistakes should be guideposts, not hitching posts." I admired his concern for young people and could understand why he had spent so many years working with Youth for Christ. I sensed a deep compassion in him for the less fortunate. And above all, I knew that his first love was the Lord and that it would always be that way. I had a love for children, too. But was there something else in my past that had stirred a desire in me to work with them?

And then I remembered. In school, teachers often asked me to help them work with other students. I had a natural knack for relating to children. But there were two girls in my class who seemed to always resent and even hate me. Regardless of what I did, they had it in for me. Maybe it was because one of these girls was very overweight, whereas I was always petite; today I'm still only 4 feet 10 inches tall.

One of the boys who lived near these girls became a sort of guardian for me through the years. Often he would jump between them and me and tell them to leave me alone. But one day he wasn't around to protect me, and neither was anyone else.

The overweight girl got me where no one could see us and pushed me to the ground. Then she sat on me and tickled me until I was choking and could hardly breathe and I thought I would die. If someone hadn't discovered us, I might have suffocated. As it was, I ran home and collapsed. I became very sick and frightened, unable to attend school for many days. The teacher came to the house and apologized to me and my parents, and the girls were severely reprimanded and warned never to come near me again.

But I felt sadness in my heart for a long time. I wondered what it was that made the girls so hateful. I would have liked to help them; I would have been a good friend to them. Now, as I reflected on all this, I came to understand that God had put a love in my heart for those who needed to know about Him. There was a call upon my life, and I would be true to it. I remember my father saying to me after this troublesome time, "What is God saying to you, Midge? What is God doing in your life?"

Always conscientious, I became even more so. My poetry from those days reflects where I was coming from and the direction I hoped to go. One such short poem reminds me even now of those learning days:

> *People need your forgiveness*
> *Your words of encouragement sweet*
> *You'll find those people if you look—*
> *Perhaps they're 'neath your feet.*

To this I added: "Forgiveness is the fragrance the blossom leaves on the sole after it has crushed the flower."

I wanted to please the Lord, to live as one of His children.

***

Reflections on Chapter 5

In this chapter you reflect on childhood memories. The moments you choose to share with your readers are varied, and yet there is a common thread to them. You describe this time as your "learning days." Although there are years when we acquire knowledge—including knowledge about ourselves—do we, in fact, ever stop learning?

No, we never stop learning if we listen well to what is being said, whether by teachers, preachers, other adults, or children. Paul and I try not to talk too much, but we listen and absorb what may be beneficial to us as individuals or as a couple. We often analyze a conversation or write down some points that may help the other person solve a problem. We are sometimes surprised to be asked to counsel others. Often we find that others just need us to listen to them; they come up with the answers after we have prayed with them and for them. We have always tried to hear the voices of children, and we feel sad when we see adults who don't hear the children laughing or crying. We have had to learn the language of children over the years.

Chapter 6

BEACH WALK

In all their distress he too was distressed,
and the angel of his presence saved them.
In his love and mercy he redeemed them;
he lifted them up and carried them
all the days of old.

—Isaiah 63:9

Paul had been invited to speak at a youth retreat at a camp north of Kingston, more than a hundred miles east of Toronto, on the Canadian Thanksgiving weekend. He'd called and asked if I would accompany him and play the piano for the meetings. I'd happily accepted.

I was living outside of Tillsonburg and teaching school in Ingersoll. After work on Friday afternoon

I drove to my sister's apartment west of Toronto, where Paul and I had agreed to rendezvous.

I wasn't prepared for what happened. I arrived first. I was in the bedroom, adding some things to my suitcase for the weekend in Kingston, when Paul walked in, hugged and kissed me, and then made a declaration. "I love you, and I know you love me. I have something for you."

Out came the little box every girl dreams of someday seeing in the hand of the man she loves. He opened it and there, nestled in velvet, was a sparkling diamond ring. Reaching for my hand, he said, "Can I put it on your finger?"

Shock registered on my face. Paul says it was at first sheer delight but that it quickly turned to almost sheer terror. I started to cry. "My parents don't know!" I was an old-fashioned young woman in many respects and was accustomed to doing things in a very traditional way. I knew my parents loved Paul, but were they ready to welcome him into the family as a future son-in-law? If they knew all of Paul's background, would they really approve? Besides, we hadn't gone together very long. It was all so sudden!

Paul was trying to console and convince me at the same time. "Margie, it will all work out. Your parents like me. Your dad and I hit it off so well."

As it turned out, the ring was a size six, much too large for my size-four finger. Paul slipped it on, and then we stood there laughing at the way it flopped around. "I'll speak to your parents and get your father's consent when we get back." He cupped my chin in his hands. "Does that make you feel better?"

I nestled against him. He was like a big, cuddly teddy bear. "Paul, you know I love you. But yes, I want you to ask my dad for my hand. I guess I'm hopelessly sentimental."

I put the ring back in the box and slipped it into my purse. Then we were on our way to Echo Lake conference grounds, near Kingston. As we drove, I kept taking the ring out and admiring it, then putting it back in my purse, and I went on doing this—bringing it out and putting it away—for many miles. En route, we discussed some of the obstacles that might confront us in the days ahead. How would we handle them? Neither of us came from an affluent family, and our paychecks were all we had to survive on. Like most young people, we usually had more month left than money.

It was a gorgeous time of year. The autumn leaves had been falling from the maple trees, which were dressed in their finest yellow and orange, and the sumacs were the brightest red I'd ever seen. We marveled at the beautiful foliage, and I told Paul that fall was my favorite season.

We were to meet several carloads of people at Kingston for dinner before caravanning north to Echo Lake, some twenty miles farther. We were early. As we drove along, on an impulse I said, "Let's go for a walk on the beach." We had been watching the yachts passing back and forth, making waves, and the beach looked inviting. Paul parked the car and we jumped out, leaving behind our shoes, and went off, barefoot, squishing the warm sand between our toes as we ran along.

We laughed at the gulls as they swooped down, scooping up fish in their sharp beaks. They were so graceful soaring through the air, and I remember thinking, "Free as a bird."

The setting sun dancing on the water made it sparkle. It was incredibly beautiful. As we strolled along, arms around each other's waists, we picked up our conversation where we had left off. "How do you think I should approach your father?" Paul asked. We bounced suggestions off each other.

"We've had so many weddings in our family recently," I pointed out. "Both my sister and my brother. I'm not so certain my parents are going to be ready for the idea of another wedding, even if it is next summer."

"How would you feel about the end of June or early July?" Paul asked.

As we talked, we'd grab each other's hands and dash in and out of the water as the waves rolled up on shore, leaving bubbles at our feet. Finally Paul looked at his watch and said it was time to turn back.

We laughed and made some more light talk, retracing our steps toward the car, and then, when we picked up our discussion again, it took a sudden serious turn. The waves were washing up over our footprints, leaving only one set of prints visible. Observing this, I said, "Maybe that's what will happen to us—maybe we'll be all washed up. Maybe our dreams are all going to wash away."

"No," Paul protested, "this makes me think of our future. On our wedding day, we two will become one, and oh, the joy that will be mine in going with you throughout our life together. See our footprints just up ahead? They're still there. Where they got washed out is just the troubled waters we're going to face. Every marriage faces that."

I was still apprehensive. "Will we have what it takes to weather the troubled waters?"

Paul stopped, looked deep into my eyes, and promised me, "We'll have it. If we love each other enough to fight for what we have, we'll make it. I've gone through enough, Margie, to know what fighting is all about. What we have is worth fighting for."

"What will happen when trouble comes that we just can't handle?" I stopped walking and pointed even as I asked the question. "Look, Paul, now there's only one set of footprints."

Paul sighed and was silent for a moment. His grip on my hand tightened reassuringly, and he said, "Margie, when the most troublesome times come, times that neither one of us can handle, that's when the Lord will carry us both, as long as we maintain our faith and trust in Him."

It was such a beautiful thought, expressed with such utmost sincerity that it momentarily took my breath away. "Ohhh," I remember saying, "that's wonderful." The poet in me stirred. How could I let this man go? Yet love demanded so much. Could I risk loving him with all my heart?

Then he playfully picked me up, swinging me into the air and saying, "See, like this."

I squealed and cried out, "I can't see you, I can't see you!" We were young and in love, serious and contemplative, but it was to be a happy outing and Paul felt the need to hear me laugh and make me smile. He knew that things had been difficult for me since I'd been hit by the bolt of lightning, that I still wasn't completely well and was on medication. I needed this weekend retreat as much as any of the students who would be attending. As he twirled me around in the air, I squealed some more.

"I'm here," he laughed, "I'm holding you, you're safe."

It all happened in the space of just a few minutes, but the impression it made lasted and will last forever. I remember how Paul gently put me down, how he kissed me tenderly. I remember how we kept walking, arms around each other's waists. But as we walked, we continued to silently observe our two sets of footprints—and sometimes only one. And it set my mind to musing. I was quite absorbed in my thinking, almost to the point of abstraction.

We returned to the Holiday Inn, where we were to meet the others. As we sat in the restaurant, waiting for them to arrive, I took a paper napkin and began jotting down some ideas and phrases.

"What are you doing?" Paul asked, as if he didn't already know. He'd become quite accustomed to my reaching for something to write on whenever we were together. Poems were always forming in my head, it seemed.

"Oh, just another poem." I smiled at him. "About our footprints in the sand."

He reached across the table, patting my hand. He loved my poetry and was always expressing surprise and appreciation. He was a great encourager.

Following dinner, we all piled back into our cars and drove on to Echo Lake. We found our cabins, unpacked our belongings, said our goodnights, and settled in for the evening. The girls in our cabin were giggling and having fun, but I found it difficult to join in. I was glad when they settled down and one by one fell asleep. Yet sleep eluded me.

I thought about the diamond ring in the box. I wondered if Paul's and my relationship had proceeded too fast. We'd known each other only six weeks. What would my family say? My mind replayed our beach-walk conversation. And then I reached for my notepad, pen, and flashlight. The words that had been forming in my head since that afternoon began taking shape on the paper.

As if in a dream, I saw a story unfolding in my mind's eye. I saw myself walking along a beach with the Lord, our feet leaving footprints in the sand. Across the sky flashed scenes from my life, and for each scene I noticed two sets of footprints in the sand—my own and that of the Lord. When the last scene of my life shot before me, I looked back and saw that there was only one set of footprints. I realized that this was at the lowest and saddest times of my life. I asked the Lord where He had been when I needed Him most.

The words tumbled out, easily, effortlessly.

"Lord, You told me when I decided to follow You,
You would walk and talk with me all the way.
But I'm aware that during the most troublesome
times of my life there is only one set of footprints.

I just don't understand why, when I needed You
most,
    You leave me."

Then I wrote his reply.

He whispered, "My precious child,
I love you and will never leave you,
never, ever, during your trials and testings.
When you saw only one set of footprints
it was then that I carried you."

Suddenly I was aware that I was writing free verse, which was not at all usual for me. I was accustomed to writing in rhyming verse or couplets.

I looked at my watch. It was 3 a.m. I shivered, feeling the cool early morning air. You'd better get some shut-eye, I told myself, or you won't be worth anything the rest of the day. Just before falling asleep I thought, Now I've written this and I don't even have a title. Then I wondered, Has this just been a dream?

In the morning, upon awakening, I reached for the notepad, read the poem, and immediately the thought came: You should call it "I Had a Dream."

And that's how I wrote the poem that the nurse read to my husband in his hospital bed so many years later. It came to be known by the title "Footprints," but to us it will always be a reminder of our beach walk. To us it symbolizes the time when we realized that God was saying that this would be a God-blessed marriage, and that He would always be there walking with us, carrying us when we needed to be carried—as, of course, He wants to do for all His children.

***

Reflections on Chapter 6

"The words that had been forming in my head since that afternoon began taking shape on the paper . . . As if in a dream, I saw a story unfolding in my mind's eye. I saw myself walking along a beach with the Lord, our feet leaving footprints in the sand." That was in 1964. At that moment in time, as you began to write your poem, did you have a glimmer of an idea of the impact that your words would have—did you ever

imagine that they would reach so many people, in so many places throughout the world?

I had no idea of the impact this writing would have. It was written in the dark of the night and given as a special gift to my boyfriend, to remember the particular weekend in October 1964 when he asked me to marry him. We are still astounded to realize it reaches so many people throughout the world, even in remote places. We believe people have attended conferences that we have been at, have heard the poem and loved it, and have shared it with someone. They don't always know who the writer is, but they are anxious to share the messages of the poem: He will never leave us or forsake us; and He walks with us. These are very simple but true messages that warm the heart. Some people even think the poem comes directly from the Bible, and try to find it there.

Chapter 7

"I Had a Dream"

God has said, "Never will I leave you;
never will I forsake you."

—Hebrews 13:5

The weather was perfect that memorable fall weekend. Chipmunks ran freely around the grounds searching for food, and squirrels were filling their cheeks with nuts and hiding them in trees in preparation for the winter to come. We enjoyed watching them. The sun shone, and the leaves glowed, and the whole scene was breathtakingly beautiful.

The next morning, according to our plan, I was the pianist for the retreat meetings. Paul delivered a message entitled "I Cannot Pray the Lord's

Prayer." About a hundred young people from all over Ontario were there—teenagers from high schools, along with college students and young career people. Paul explained what had happened when he worked for Youth for Christ and "borrowed" money without telling anyone, and how he had found himself unable to pray—God had seemed distant. He spoke of how unworthy he had felt because he knew he'd failed God had and those who trusted him.

I watched as the young people listened intently. "I couldn't say, 'Our Father who art in heaven,'" he confessed. Then he told them about his own father—about the abuse he'd suffered at his hands, and how he finally had learned to love him after hating him and wanting to kill him for so many years. It was obvious to me that God was using the worst thing that had happened in Paul's life to show these young people the Lord's mercy and loving Fatherliness.

I showed Paul the poem "I Had a Dream" that afternoon. "Paul, God has quieted my heart. My father isn't going to reject you when you ask him if you can marry me. That experience yesterday on the beach, and then writing this, have given me courage. God really did something very special for us yesterday—he gave us a beautiful visual lesson. God's promise to always be with us is the only possible way our marriage will work."

As Paul read the poem, he understood what I was talking about, and he asked if he could read it at the evening retreat service. His message to the young people was that God is always there for us—that, though unseen, He is with us to care for us and carry us through. The words he spoke made an impact. The audience sat spellbound. "When Margie and I walked along the beach, discussing our coming marriage, at one point I swooped her up and held her up high," he told the young listeners. "She laughed and protested, but she knew I had a hold on her, a firm grip that would not let go." Then Paul made his words very personal for each of the listeners. "It's the same with all of us. We can't see Jesus, but He guarantees in His Word that while we were sinners He died for us. That's His guarantee. You can't see Him, but He's there . . . believe that! There were many times when I seemed to be in utter darkness and I couldn't see

Him. I was flailing and lashing out, and sometimes I didn't think He could still love me, but always He was there, carrying me. And that's what He will do for you, too."

Then he read the poem. Later, several people told us you could have heard the proverbial pin drop as many young people made life-changing decisions about trusting Christ with their lives.

The next morning, many asked for copies of the poem. I also gave a copy to Lloyd Smith ("Smitty"), Paul's buddy, an outstanding musician who was going to compose a musical score for the poem as a wedding gift to us. Lloyd died shortly after that—he was fatally injured in an inner-city conflict during his missionary work—so he was never able to complete the score. It was one of those times when we knew, after later reflection, that the Lord truly carried Paul, for Smitty's death was a great personal loss.

The next morning, following that glorious retreat weekend, everyone said their good-byes and went in different directions. We stopped in Frankford for lunch and Paul introduced me to Mom and Dad Adams, his "foster" parents—the elderly couple he had been boarding with when he found Christ. Before leaving, they said a prayer with us about our new life together.

We laughed, sang, and joked all the way home. When we became weary, we turned up the radio volume to the highest level and opened the windows. Just before reaching the farm, Paul pulled to the side of the road, and we had a time of prayer together. We were both quietly serious, wondering how my dad would react to what Paul was going to ask him. After all, Paul and I had really only had two dates. Even in my own mind, the questions kept going around: Do we truly know each other? I learned more about Paul this weekend than I've known before—we're so different—can it work? Our backgrounds were exactly the opposite in every possible way.

A crackling fire greeted us, and Mom and Dad were anxious to hear all about the retreat. I whispered to my mother that I needed to talk to her alone, and Paul was left standing in the kitchen, staring nervously at my father. He describes that encounter like this: "Margie's father was a big rough-hewn German farmer who was sitting there with his thumbs hooked in the bib of his overalls, looking me up and down as if I were a steer he might be considering for purchase."

My father had a wonderful sense of humor, and I think he knew all along what was coming, but he kept Paul in the hot seat for just a few moments.

"You want to talk to me?"

"Yes, sir."

"Well, did you have an accident?"

"No," Paul responded.

"Then what do you want to talk about?"

"Margie."

"What's wrong with Midge?"

"Nothing's wrong with her."

"Then what are you talking about?"

"I think I'm supposed to say, 'I would like to have your daughter's hand in marriage.'"

Paul said there was an awkward silence for what to him seemed like an eternity, but finally Dad said, "Well, what's wrong with the rest of her?" and he was grinning from ear to ear.

"All right, I'd like all of her," Paul said, grinning back.

My father wanted to know if Paul really loved me and told him he'd better know. "She's my little girl, and I've taken good care of her all these years. Will you do the same? You must love her in good and bad times, and love her even more than you love yourself."

Paul gave a wonderful response to the earlier grilling and to my father's sentimental statements: "Mr. Fishback, I will love Margie and I will honor her. I will try to make her life happy. But I'm not stupid. There are times when she's going to be unhappy. And when she's hurt, I will be there to comfort her. I don't want to take her away from your family, but I want her to be my wife. I want to belong to your family!"

The next thing Paul knew, my dad got to his feet, put his big, callused hands on Paul's shoulders, and gave him a bone-crushing hug. "C'm'ere, son . . . let me welcome you to the family!"

And that's how my mother and I found the two of them. There was a lot of hugging going on in that old-fashioned kitchen that night. Then we all sat down and I shared with them the poem and our experience as we'd walked along the beach. My parents were deeply touched and immediately saw the significance of what had taken place.

I told them about my sleepless night and how in the early morning hours it had seemed that God was in control of my hand and the pen as I wrote. "God impressed upon my heart two verses from the Bible," I said. "Here, let me read them to you." And I read Isaiah 63:9 and Hebrews 13:5.

The Isaiah passage says, "In all their distress he too was distressed, and the angel of his presence saved them. In his love and mercy he redeemed them; he lifted them up and carried them all the days of old."

And Hebrews 13:5 states: "Keep your lives free from the love of money and be content with what you have, because God has said, 'Never will I leave you; never will I forsake you.'"

Father gave us his blessing, and we made our wedding plans in the months that followed. We were able to see each other on only two special occasions before our wedding date of July 10, 1965.

***

Reflections on Chapter 7

I love the story about Paul telling your dad, "I would like to have your daughter's hand in marriage." After Paul waited in the "hot seat," for what seemed like an eternity, your father at last replied, "Well, what's wrong with the rest of her?" Your dad surely broke the ice! That story made me laugh. Do you think you inherited your father's wonderful sense of humor? How important do you feel laughter is in our lives?

I had not analyzed it, but Paul has always felt that I have inherited my father's rather dry sense of humor. He often says, "That would be just like your dad"—and then laughs. Laughter has had such a major role in our lives. I used to write poems and puppet scripts with lots of humor. It is so important. This past year has been the first time in our marriage that laughter has not been as frequent and fluid on a daily basis, and I have felt some stress creeping in when I could previously laugh things off and not take a situation so seriously. The reason there hasn't been as much laughter is that Paul suffered heart problems again, and I think we were concentrating on what the doctors would be able to do for him. As a result, in December 2010, he had a pacemaker and defibrillator installed at St. Paul's Hospital in Vancouver, British Columbia. He has come through a year of recovery to a healthy heart, thanks to many medical professionals who were concerned for him. Our children and grand-children took up playing more table games as a result of Paul's illness and we enjoyed laugh-ter—along with popcorn and peanuts—in those quieter times.

Laughter was so important to me that I wrote this little poem when I was a young girl. It is called "Sunshine and Music." I think it is just as important today as it was then. My Scripture was Psalm 100, and our daughter Tina still sings the psalm with her ventriloquist doll, Ashley.

Laughter is just like sunshine
It freshens all the day,
It tips the peak of life with light
And drives the clouds away;
The soul grows glad that hears it

And feels its courage strong:
A laugh is just like sunshine
For cheering folks along.

A laugh is just like music
It lingers in the heart,
And where its melody is heard
The ills of life depart.
And happy thoughts come crowding
Its joyful notes to greet;
A laugh is just like music
For making living sweet.

It is easier to laugh than frown, and it takes less energy! I have to remind myself of this lesson learned even today, when we forget to smile or laugh. Even large corporations are finding that an upbeat mentality is essential to their employees' health needs.

Part Four—Change

Be strong and courageous. Do not be afraid or terrified . . . for the Lord your God goes with you.

—*Deuteronomy 31:6*

Chapter 8

"A New Life"

It's a new life, oh, how He changed me,
A new life, He rearranged me,
A new life, richer and fuller,
A wonderful, wonderful life.

I also wrote a new song that weekend at the retreat, which was introduced there. The words speak of the new life in Christ—deeper and wider, greater and more wonderful than the old life; little did Paul and I know the full meaning those words would have in our lives as man and wife. Time after time we would be made to realize how fragile life is and how dependent man is on God.

We had a great honeymoon week, going to Kingston and retracing our "footsteps" walk, this time sharing the confidence that our step of commitment had given both of us.

Then it was back to Toronto. Paul was still managing film rentals at the Christian bookstore, and I began teaching in a school in the Yorkville district, at that time a rather tough neighborhood in the heart of Toronto. Weekends found us doing presentations for youth groups. Paul's "Gospel Magic with a Message," a magician show tied in to biblical messages, was a big attraction. We were kept very busy.

From almost the first day we were married, Paul had serious health problems. He had had rheumatic fever as a child after his mother died and had spent about a year in a brace. The disease had left him with a weakened heart. Sometimes I found it hard to be patient with his weakness.

In November, after four months of marriage, I called my mother with another complaint: "Every time I cook something, Paul ends up getting sick. Here I am taking gourmet cooking classes, and he gets sick."

"What are you putting in your cooking?" my mother asked.

"Lots of spices," I told her.

"Why are you using all those spices?" she asked.

"Mom, I got this beautiful, gigantic spice-rack set for a wedding gift. I have to use those spices. They're wonderful!"

"They aren't so wonderful if they make your husband sick. You've got to make a decision—either you cook your own meals using your spices and cook Paul's meals separately, or you cook in order for Paul to survive and be well so the two of you can enjoy your married life. My dear, you've got to make up your mind—for better or for worse!" And down went the receiver.

Everything seemed to be working against me. To me, cooking was one of the central things about being married. Good cooking, fellowship—these were important to a marriage. I tried baking—no success. Failure after failure. I despaired. Finally, with every cake turning out like Jell-O, Paul got around to looking at the oven—and, of course, it wasn't working properly. I couldn't help but blame him for all those ruined desserts—why hadn't he guessed that the oven was the problem?

At one point Paul was so sick with a serious ear

infection that he became delirious, and my brother Jim ended up taking care of him while I worked. When I came home, I found a note saying Paul had been taken to the hospital. I had to get compassionate in a hurry. I was getting ready to go to the hospital when my brother brought Paul home, and I could see he really had a high fever. "You must get up in the middle of the night and look after him," Jim instructed me. "See to it that he gets his pills when he needs to take them."

I dutifully gave Paul his medicine, had him drink lots of water, and held his hand. In the morning, my brother came over and said, "Now, Margie, I want to show you how to change his dressing."

I protested. I knew what a mess his ear was, and I was squeamish. "Look, he's your husband," Jimmy said. I learned to change the dressing, but I wasn't happy about it.

We didn't go home for Christmas that first year of our marriage. I knew I had to get a handle on my emotions, and I realized shamefully that I had been a failure in our marriage thus far. I was a very fussy house fanatic—thinking I had to keep our apartment just so. Nurturing our relationship was taking second place to the adjustments of marriage. Thankfully, I came to my senses and began to focus on my husband and the ministry God had entrusted to us.

We got into children's ministry quite by accident—at least, that's the way it seemed to us, but we know, of course, that nothing is happenstance with God. Paul had been invited to speak for a week at a church in Timmins, more than four hundred miles north of Toronto. When he walked into the church on the first night, he was shocked to see it full of little kids. He was accustomed to speaking to teenagers. Then he found out what had happened—a flyer advertising his visit had a misprint. Instead of inviting youth "15 to 21," the flier said "5 to 12"!

As it turned out, it was a wonderful week, with Paul demonstrating illusions, rope and handkerchief tricks, phantom-box tricks, a "Bible tear" trick, and other object lessons, all demonstrating biblical truths in memorable ways. I hadn't gone along to Timmins, but I was aware of the flyer mix-up because Paul phoned me right after the first meeting. That had sent me to my knees to pray, and I'd enlisted the help of two other teachers as well. When Paul returned home and told me what had taken place with the children and how they had enjoyed his program, I wasn't surprised. God does answer prayer. "Paul, you'd make a great children's worker," I told him.

At first he objected, but then he began to see that God had given him a heart for children. He realized in the months that followed, as he became more and more involved with children, that God had been putting him in touch with an entire generation that was desperately trying to find alternatives to isolation. Many of these were latchkey kids—with working moms and dads, if they were lucky enough to have both—and they knew about loneliness.

Together Paul and I confronted what was becoming very obvious to us—together we made a team, because my interest as a teacher was with younger children.

Nine months later, we knew it was time for Paul to leave the bookstore and step out on his own in the film-rental business. We became the new Toronto representatives, not only of Gospel Films but of most of the other major studios producing Christian films at that time. Paul also began doing more traveling, working with the well-known country-and-western singer and Hollywood personality Redd Harper.

I was trying to hold down a full-time teaching position and travel with Paul when possible. We were entertaining children all over the country. In particular, Paul was being asked to appear in purely secular magic shows during the winter months—January through March—at some of the biggest amusement parks in the United States, including Six Flags Magic Mountain in Atlanta; Busch Gardens in Florida; Knott's Berry Farm, the Japanese Tea Gardens, and the Crocodile Farm, all in the Los Angeles area; Disneyland in southern California; and Disney World in Florida.

In the summer, when I was on vacation from teaching and the film business was slow, we concentrated on ministry in churches, camps, and daily vacation Bible schools in and around Toronto.

This routine took its toll, however, and I knew I had to make a choice. Should I continue to hold down a full-time teaching position or should I resign and travel with Paul?

***

Reflections on Chapter 8

This is a chapter that starts with a decision. As the chapter ends, you make an important choice. You say that you and Paul found yourselves in children's ministry quite by accident—at least, that's the way it seemed at first. Then you explain that nothing is happenstance with God. Could you please elaborate on what you mean by that?

I was trained as a classroom and music teacher in the school system. Paul, on the other hand, worked with teens and young adults—some street kids, and also prisoners—and he thought we would start to develop a recovery program for the City of Toronto, either through our home church and community or through Youth for Christ. At the time, Paul had little patience with younger children. He thought they should be seen and not heard, and he didn't think they had the capacity to comprehend important life-changing matters. He assumed I was interested

98

in children only because I was a schoolteacher, and he thought I probably wouldn't be interested in making working with kids a life's work. But people change. Still, I am always amazed that we have worked around the globe for forty-five years in children's ministry.

Chapter 9

"Letter from a Friend"

*I am writing to say how much I care for you and
how much I want you to know me better.*

F aced with the choice of whether to continue
teaching or to travel with my husband, I chose
the latter. It was on one of our trips, in July 1966,
that God got my attention in a most dramatic way.
It happened on a Pennsylvania turnpike in the
United States.

We were returning from a vacation and afterwards
attending the International Audio Visual Convention
when we found ourselves caught in a tornado.
Animals were being blown away, and we watched,
horror-stricken, as a van we'd been following, loaded
with nuns, was blown right off the hill. There was no

way we could stop, and although we later reported the accident, we never heard what happened to the nuns. It was all Paul could do to keep the car on the road. We finally found protection under an overpass.

The next day, still very shaken by the experience and our near brush with death, I sat down, pen in hand, and these words came out on paper:

Letter from a Friend

I am writing to say how much I care
for you and how much I want you
to know me better.
When you awoke this morning, I exploded
a brilliant sunrise through your window
trying to get your attention. You rushed off.
Later, I spotted you walking and talking
with some friends. I bathed you in
warm sunshine. I perfumed the air
with nature's sweet scent. You rushed off.
You didn't notice me.
Then I shouted to you in a tornado.
I painted you a beautiful rainbow
in the sky. Then you gave me a glance.

Still you rushed off.
That evening I spilled moonbeams
in your face. I sent a cool breeze
to rest you and take away your fear.
I watched over you as you slept. I shared
your thoughts. You were faintly aware
I was so near. I've chosen you. I have
a special task for you. I hope you will
talk to me soon. Only I brought you through
the storm. Others saw no morn.
I remain near. I am your friend.
I love you very much.

Your Friend, Jesus

I read the poem to Paul, and we discussed its meaning. Our lives were on a fast track and we knew it. Did we need to slow down? Did we need to stop, to think about where we were headed? Did we need to get off altogether?

We didn't change our ways for a while. At first, the "winter vacations" to the United States and the long-distance traveling were enjoyable, and I liked the fast-paced routine. I traveled with Paul throughout the winter and spring of 1968, right up to the time we had a little one of our own.

Christina (Tina) was born on Victoria Day, 1968. I wasn't well, and my mother came and stayed with us. It seemed that I had built up some kind of immunity to pain and had a violent reaction to medication—like an epileptic seizure—when Tina was born. My heart actually stopped. Doctors thought that I had suffered from spinal meningitis after being struck by lightning five years earlier, and they warned me that I could expect to have some health problems from this about every seven years. I was warned against becoming overly fatigued or being under too much stress.

We had a beautiful baby, however, and once I was back on my feet, this new little life drew out the mothering instincts in me, and Paul became a wonderful father. The following summer, I once again joined Paul in his travels, this time with a baby in tow.

It was in 1970 that I finally really began to admit that our lives were headed in the wrong direction. Paul was making good money performing at the secular jobs, but we weren't getting ahead financially.

I could see that our film business was suffering as we left it in the hands of college students; we just weren't "minding the store" at home enough. I was also concerned that Paul had become somewhat cynical about Christian ministry. In some respects, he was justified—churches often didn't pay on time, nor did they begin to match what he could receive in the secular world. His bitterness about the way churches sometimes treated outside speakers such as ourselves began to show.

Our second daughter, Paula, was born in January 1971. Another new life.

The years were going by so fast, and it seemed that our own lives were unraveling at the same speed. With two little ones to care for, I found myself staying home and resenting it when I did have to join Paul in some city, usually in the United States. We had a beautiful home in Don Mills, one of the nicer neighborhoods in the northern part of Toronto. We had a swimming pool, a couple of late-model cars, and credit cards that we used often. But we didn't have a normal family life.

The tension between Paul and me increased. We seemed to be slipping farther and farther apart.

It was on a return trip from Warsaw, Indiana, where we had been at a Ken Anderson film conference, that Paula, then about three years old, got my attention. We were walking through an airport when she sat down right in the middle of nowhere and couldn't go on. She was one sick little girl; she had contracted scarlet fever. Paul hoisted her on his shoulders and we walked on. I had an instant flashback to the beach walk and the footprints in the sand, and knew that God was still carrying us along, but that it was time to get back in step with Him.

It was as if I heard God say, "You keep rushing off . . . I hope you will talk to me soon."

***

Reflections on Chapter 9

You and Paul are blessed with the birth of your two daughters: Tina in 1968 and Paula in 1971. These should be the most splendid moments for a family. Yet at the same time, you sense your lives are headed in the wrong direction. As the chapter ends, Paul hoists an ill Paula onto his shoulders, and you have an instant flashback to the walk on the beach and the footprints in the sand. At that moment, you understood it was time to get back in step with God. How did you know this precisely?

This moment happened in California, when ego, pride, and popularity had slowly and subtly seeped into our lives. I knew it without a doubt when one evening our close friend—a famous entertainer—had finished a marvelous show and invited us to come and relax with him and his wife. During this casual get-together, our friend became completely drunk and shared the deep disappointment he felt about his marriage and children. Needless to say, we had a sleepless night. The next day, I started to evaluate and review the situation, and I realized that we were getting very far away from our spiritual value system in life. I commented to Paul that "what the Lord gives us makes us feel better, but what the devil gives us makes us feel bitter." The verse in Jeremiah 31:3 came to me very clearly: The Lord appeared to him, saying, "I have loved you with an everlasting love; I have drawn you with loving-kindness." I knew then that it was time to return to Canada and direct our minds, and our hearts, to a life's work that would have lasting value for time and eternity—not just until beauty, fame, and talent fade away.

Chapter 10

TRIALS AND TESTINGS

During your trials and testings,
when you saw only one set of footprints
it was then that I carried you.

The decision was made. No more traipsing around the United States doing magic acts in secular settings for the Powers family. I had been praying for a long time that we would get out of the Hollywood kind of life we'd been in for too many years. A verbal battle, waged on a Los Angeles freeway while we were trying to maneuver our way through Friday-night traffic, precipitated this decision.

We'd been invited to meet friends for dinner, but something inside me exploded en route. "I'm leaving you and taking the girls with me!"

Paul was stunned, but so was I at this unexpected outburst. Somehow we got through the dinner hour, and on the way back to Redd Harper's home, where we were staying, we were able to talk out our situation. We loved each other, we had precious children, we were God's children, and we had a great ministry. "All of that should come first, Paul," I gently reminded him. That night, we prayed and entrusted ourselves and the future to God. We also asked our good friend Redd to pray for us, so that we might understand the direction our lives should go.

Upon our return to Toronto, we were confronted with an enormous stack of bills. "Please handle it, Margie," Paul said. "You know I'm not good at it." Yes, I did know, but what a struggle it proved to be. Together we plunged into our summer ministry work, but it was a troublesome time—a time of trial and testing the likes of which we'd never experienced before.

The franchise film industry was experiencing a major slump, and we were urged to sell the business. Still we hung on, hoping for a holiday upswing, but as we headed into fall and the holiday season it didn't materialize. Christmas 1972 looked bleak.

Hitting rock bottom was something neither of us had anticipated when we had told God we'd put Him first and give up the other lifestyle. Poverty? I couldn't believe it.

I urged Paul to go out and try to collect some of the money that eight churches in the Toronto area owed us for fall children's crusades. None had paid him at the time he spoke. It proved to be the most humiliating day of his life, netting not quite forty dollars.

Discouraged, Paul handed the money to me upon his return so I could go out and get groceries. "Spend it carefully, Margie," he cautioned, "it's all we've got. I've put gas in the car for the trip to the farm." We were planning to drive to my parents' farm the next morning to spend Christmas Day with the family.

The girls were bundled up, and we left to go shopping. Two hours later we returned. I felt good about some bargains I'd found, but Paul was angry, especially when Tina showed him a roll of gold wrapping paper. His frustration boiled up and spewed out as he screamed at me for being so wasteful. The atmosphere at dinner was depressing, and we picked at our food. Little Tina's tearful blue eyes mirrored the pain we were all feeling.

Paul and I went to his downstairs office to do some gift wrapping. Tina was trying to help. At one point Paul sarcastically said, "Tina, would you go upstairs and get that gold paper your mother wasted the money on?"

If I hadn't felt cut down to size before, I certainly did then. Tina took her time about coming back, so Paul stormed up the stairs. I was on his heels. There sat Tina, in an alcove just off the living room, surrounded by wads of gold paper and three pairs of scissors. Gobs of sticky tape were all over her, as well as the rug. And the single sheet of gold paper? She'd used it all trying to wrap something that looked like a shoebox.

Anger flooded Paul's face as he raced across the room, grabbed her by one arm, and jerked her into the air, slapping her hard several times. Tina's screams and sobs made him realize what he was doing, and he stopped, letting go of her so that she fell to the floor, a terrified, crying little girl.

I was in shock. Was this the Paul who claimed to love God and little children?

For Paul it was a flashback to his own childhood, when he had been so abused at the hands of his raging, drunken father. Later, he confessed that all he could think for the rest of the evening was *You're just like your father . . . you're a coward who beats little children . . . just like your father . . . you're no good, no good, no good . . .*

I put Tina to bed, comforting her as best I could.

The next morning, as we prepared to go to the farm, Paul tripped and almost fell over the box Tina had wrapped in the gold paper. Still irritated, he kicked it out of the way, but at that moment Tina ran to the box, picked it up, and ran back to Paul. "Here, Daddy, it's for you," she whispered.

Paul took it and shook it gently, but it was very light and nothing rattled inside. The tape all over the box made it hard to unwrap, and his frustration and impatience once again spilled over. He ripped the top of the box open, but when he looked inside, there was nothing there. With his temper no longer in check, he said sharply, "Christina! Don't you know you should put something in a box before you wrap it up as a gift?"

Tears were streaming down her little face as she said, "But, Daddy, I did put something in it. I blew kisses into it! It's full of love just for you!"

An empty box, but strangely, wonderfully full. It was the gift Paul needed the most. Right there in the hallway, he dropped to his knees, hugged Tina, begged her forgiveness, and then hugged Paula and me, begging our forgiveness as well. His sobs were deep, coming from the depths of his being.

Paul received a healing within at that moment—the enemy, his anger, died. He cried out to God for help and received it.

But I had been wrong, too. I'd been upset and nagging at him. "I helped cause all of this, Paul," I confessed, "but we love each other and I know God's going to help us."

We still have that golden box. A reminder of one of the best Christmases we've ever had. It had been a time of trial and testing, but God had carried us through.

***

Reflections on Chapter 10

There is an image from this chapter that stays with the reader: "An empty box, but strangely, wonderfully full. It was the gift Paul needed the most." You still have that golden box and say that it's a reminder of one of the best Christmases you've had. What are some of the things you think about when you look at it, all these years later?

Putting my thoughts on paper for this chapter was probably the most difficult writing experience I have ever had. I remember a number of times when the tears flooded down my cheeks to the point where I would have to leave the work for a day and start again the following morning. I was putting it on the computer at that time, and twice I lost the entire day's work and went to my bedroom and locked the door. It was very upsetting to Paul when this happened the second time, and I wondered if it was worth sharing with readers this deep distress that I had suffered. Now, as I look back, I realize that even after thirteen years had gone by, I wrote a poem about that incident and how it had left an indelible mark on my mind. Needless to say, I try to keep my emotions in check. This is sometimes difficult, but we have to consider and protect our loved ones who are emotionally involved with us. (My poem "The Golden Box" appears in the poetry section at the back of this book.)

I am turning the rest of the response to this question over to Paul, who writes:

There are multiple images that flash into my mind every time I see the golden box on my desk—or share the story of the golden box. I suppose my first response was shock and horror. How could I sink so low as to be abusive (as my own father was) and to revert back to my unsettled and sad childhood? How could I possibly resort to this behavior toward one of the three most treasured gifts in my life? It was even at such a special time of year, when we think of love, hope, and joy, along with gift sharing.

I also think about compassion. When visiting children's hospital wards, we have witnessed the physical, emotional, and spiritual abuse that little ones have suffered. We always recoil from this image, and it leaves its imprint on our hearts.

The look in my daughter's eyes showed her complete love and forgiveness. This response astounded me. I still see this look of forgiveness, and Tina has said, "Dad, you have to let the memory go and just remember my love for you." God removes the sting.

Also flashing into my mind is the thought of love, which reminds us of how God's great salvation has won our hearts. I had to keep reminding myself that He had forgiven me.

After this event occurred, I studied, as did my wife, how to properly discipline children in a kindly way, as Margaret believed that verbal abuse was the beginning in a downward slide to further types of abuse. It needs to be nipped in the bud. I am reminded again that, when we seek God's forgiveness, He removes the guilt and shame of sin and restores the soul, as in the story of how King David cried out "Restore to me the joy of your salvation" (Psalm 51:12) or as in the parable of the prodigal son in Luke 15:15–20.

Chapter 11

Wings

How priceless is your unfailing love!
Both high and low among men
find refuge in the shadow of your wings.
                                          —Psalm 36:7

Angels! Our little girls knew about angels. For one thing, in the winter we loved lying down in the snow, spreading our arms, and making angels with wings. Of course, we told them about angels, too, introducing them at a very young age to Bible stories that spoke of them as "ministering spirits" for God's people. But one summer we came to know about angels in a very real way.

When our daughter Paula was just beginning to talk, soon after turning two, we headed for a crusade north of Peterborough, Ontario. A friend called shortly before we left and said, "Stop by on your way. We'll picnic in the backyard."

It was a fun time. We sat in a circle in our friends' beautiful yard, our backs to the house, enjoying the picnic. Our hostess's brother came driving up on his Harley-Davidson. Instead of putting it on its kickstand, he leaned it against the house.

Paula climbed down from my lap and, unbeknownst to us, was playing around the front wheel of the motorcycle. It happened so fast. One moment she was laughing and running around, the next moment she was screaming as the motorcycle fell on top of her, crushing her with its weight.

Everyone jumped up and ran to her. The men lifted the motorcycle off her small body. It was obvious that she was in serious condition: one of the parts of the bike had punctured her head with a deep wound. Paula was screaming as Paul picked her up and ran to the car. Blood was spurting everywhere. "Oh, dear God, help us and spare her!" I cried out over and over again. Feeling panic-stricken but, incredibly, still in control, I cautioned Paul, "Keep holding your hand on her head. Press to stop the blood."

I got into the car, and Paul handed Paula to me. Her little hands were fluttering and her whole body was in shock, shaking. I wiped the blood off one of her hands, put her thumb in her mouth, and held it there, applying pressure against the roof of her mouth.

Someone immediately called the hospital, alerting them that we were on the way. The hospital immediately called the police; several cars met us, sirens blaring, while others cleared the highway. The emergency team was waiting and ready at the hospital. Paula was rushed inside.

As they examined her, the doctors asked us to step close. "Look down here, Mrs. Powers," one of them said, and I looked. It was like gazing into a deep well. "That's where the damage is. Amazing that she's alive!" I was fully aware that it was only because of God.

Had the wound been more than a few hairs closer, it would have punctured the brain. It required thirteen stitches, but we were able to take Paula home from the hospital later that evening. Both Paul and I were in absolute awe as we experienced the presence and strength of the Lord.

I put Paula in her crib and positioned myself in a chair alongside. I stayed awake, praying, thanking God for sparing the life of our precious little one. At one point I felt a coolness on my face and I moved back. Still I felt the gentle breeze. Paula whimpered just a little, opened her eyes as I bent over her, and said, "Wings, Mommy, wings."

Wings, Mommy, wings. I sat down and repeated Paula's words. She sighed a little sigh, and once again I heard her say, "Wings . . . wings."

"Oh, thank You, thank You, Lord, for what You have done!"

I breathed another prayer of gratitude for God's watchful care. A little later I went into our bedroom, awakened Paul, and told him, "Paula's guardian angels are watching over her." Then I told him what had happened.

"Let me sit with her now," he said. "You need some rest. She's going to be all right, but let me watch her now."

I agreed, lay down, and fell asleep peacefully. The last thing I remember is the gentle breeze and "Wings, Mommy, wings."

***

Reflections on Chapter 11

This chapter prompts me to ask, Does everyone have a guardian angel? And how do we know when our angel makes an appearance?

This is a delicate subject—there are some people who believe in angels and some who do not. That is their prerogative! I am from the school that believes, and I don't like to debate the subject. To me, it is a very private and sacred topic. My guardian angel has visited me on six special occasions in my life's journey—and there has been no mistaking it, as far as I am concerned. On a lighter note, maybe missionaries need their guardian angels' visitation more than others; I don't know. But it gives a reason to pray for ambassadors and military and service people—as well as missionaries—in other, often rugged and unsafe, lands.

Chapter 12

"MY ANGELS WILL HELP YOU"

For he will command his angels concerning you
to guard you in all your ways.

—*Psalm 91:11*

The motorcycle falling on little Paula was not to be our only encounter with her guardian angels. We are sure that in the summer of 1989, when she fell into the whirlpool of water and was swept over the falls, it was a true miracle that her life was spared. The odds of someone surviving a sixty-eight-foot fall like that are very slim. Paula, too, has a way of keeping her guardian angels busy.

On one occasion when our daughters were still little, friends met us at our home in Don Mills. We planned to go to the Prince Hotel for dinner. We were all chatting in the front hall, waiting for Paul. He came bounding down the stairs, reached the landing, and tripped. Everyone heard the sound—like a yardstick cracking—and we just knew he'd broken his leg. Still he insisted on going out, and there was no way anyone could persuade him otherwise. During dinner, his leg swelled incredibly. Although he tried bravely to conceal it, there was no mistaking it: something was terribly wrong, and he was in excruciating pain. He leaned heavily on our friends, Ernie and Phyllis Hayes, as we made our way out of the restaurant.

"Paul, you must have that looked at," they insisted, and this time he didn't object. We decided to go directly to the hospital from the hotel. Our friends agreed to drive the girls home, and said they'd wait there for our return.

Before parting, seven-year-old Paula said, "Daddy, I want to pray for your leg," and she laid her hands on his leg, closed her eyes, and prayed: "God, please heal our daddy's leg because he doesn't have time to be sick." Then she looked up at Paul and very confidently said, "My angels will help you, Daddy."

I drove the car to the hospital, and on the way I looked across at Paul. In spite of the pain, we couldn't help smiling at each other as we spoke of Paula's sweet and simple faith. But then he pulled his pant leg up, looked down, and said, "Margie, from the kneecap to below the ankle it's really swollen."

It took eight minutes to get from the hotel to the hospital emergency entrance. I jumped out of the car and went around to the passenger side. "Please sit here, Paul," I said, "while I go in and get a wheelchair and an attendant. Can you lift your leg out?" I asked. "Careful . . . careful," I cautioned. I stooped down to assist him, and when we pulled his pant leg up again, the swelling was no longer there. A surprised look crossed his face, then he cautiously flexed the leg while I looked on in awed silence.

"Margie! The pain . . . it's gone. I can bend it! And look! The swelling is gone!"

We looked at each other in amazement. "God answered Paula's prayer," he said quietly. "Thank You, God, and thank you, angels."

Still I insisted he go in and have the leg X-rayed. The X-rays showed nothing, not so much as a small fracture. The doctor and nurses on duty were just as shocked as we were when we told them what had happened.

All the way home we kept shaking our heads. "I can't believe it," one or the other of us would say. It wasn't that we didn't have the faith to believe that God could instantaneously knit broken bones back together, but it was just so overwhelming.

When we drove up to our house, our friends and Tina and Paula rushed out to the car. "Daddy, Daddy!" the girls shouted.

"Paul, you drove the car!" Phyllis said.

"Why are you back so soon?" Ernie asked.

"I know why," Paula said shyly, giving her daddy a big hug.

She could just as well have said "I told you so!"

***

Reflections on Chapter 12

Another great theme emerges in this chapter: the power of prayer. Could you expand on this theme for your readers?

Years ago, I used a phrase, "Prayer changes things." I believe that prayer does change situations for the good. Whether we like it or not, we are still seeing miracles because people have prayed for their loved ones. A Canadian woman lost in the Nevada outback was recently found—when it seemed impossible. A young man from Quebec who was out for a day hike and became lost for nine days was recently located on a ski mountain near where we live. These are not coincidences. "I call on the Lord in my distress, and he answers me" (Psalm 120:1). Often people pray as a last resort. I have always felt that it is better to pray first, and even on a regular basis. If you don't use that gift, you lose it. And He is in tune, listening to us and waiting for us to call on Him in our distresses. I am reminded of Luke 11:9–10, "Ask . . . seek . . . find." In your cry of distress, you sometimes wonder where to start. Just start with the Lord's Prayer. Seeking help through prayer has become much more common in the past few years. Maybe people became too self-sufficient. And perhaps now we are realizing how much we need to pray and seek God's guidance in our lives.

Chapter 13

OUT OF THE MOUTHS OF BABES

From the lips of children . . .
you have ordained praise.

—Psalm 8:2

Through the years, in our travels, Paul read my poetry on many, many occasions. Often the poems were used in church bulletins. Paul's messages—given throughout Ontario and to the farthest corner, by the Quebec border—were frequently taped.

During this time, I also wrote a lot of choruses, and we taught them as we moved about. These were catchy little songs that adults and children learned easily. In particular, the audiences seemed to enjoy singing "Do You Know?" (to the tune of

"Do-Re-Mi") and "Praise the Lord, I Know" (to the tune "It's a Small World (After All)").

In New York State, I taught "King of Kings," set to a folk tune. Paul had learned the tune on a trip he'd made to Israel, and once he was back home and had taught it to me, I wrote some lyrics for it. Also around this time, because Paul was starting to gain a little weight and the girls and I were doing what we called our "aerobic tunes," I made up a fun tune that everyone enjoyed entitled "Ho, Ho, Ho, Hosannah!" It soon became a favorite. We made a trip to the West Coast some months later and found people there already singing and teaching this catchy little chorus. "Paul, I'm happy and grateful that these choruses are moving across the country so quickly," I said.

Our girls were growing up and participating in meetings. We had given them ventriloquist dolls. Tina had named hers Cindy; Paula called hers Heather. This became their introduction to joining us in our ministry presentation. Not long after that, Paul himself got a "vent doll," as they are called in the trade, who was named TJ (for Timmy Jimmy). Later he acquired Rusty, who became his companion wherever he spoke until the day Rusty was stolen. Then, through God-orchestrated events, Andy came into Paul's possession, and became the indispensable door-opener to many places that would otherwise be unwilling to admit someone like Paul and his family. We became, in every sense of the word, a real family team.

It was during the mid-1970s, following a return trip from Israel, that Paul experienced a stress attack (called that by the doctors who attended to him). He was ordered to cut back on work and take it easy. Our film business was in decline, and when a Christian bookstore in Toronto offered to buy it, the sale was consummated. It was the same bookstore where Paul had worked in the 1960s, and now he was hired back to manage the film-rental business on a salaried basis. I helped, doing part-time work as a bookkeeper. For the next seven years we worked there, as well as continuing our ministry throughout Canada and parts of the upper United States.

"Cutting back" just didn't seem to be in our vocabulary, however—Little People's Ministry presented so many needs and opportunities that we felt we couldn't ignore. We had an annual two-month leave of absence from the bookstore in July and August to do daily vacation Bible schools in the area, and since the film business was slow then, the arrangement worked out nicely.

Overscheduling was common for us. Not that we meant to do it, but it happened. Once again, God used one of our daughters to get our attention. It happened one summer at a church in Fergus, Ontario, where we were teaching. Tina, eight at the time, participated in the programs with us. Five-year-old Paula, however, stayed at our camping trailer with a babysitter. She was a happy and contented child.

Returning to the trailer to pick up a piece of forgotten equipment one noon, Paul stopped to say hi to Paula, who was playing in the shade of a tree with a crèche he'd brought back from Israel for her. He looked down at the set and asked, "Honey, where are Mary and Joseph? I don't see them."

"Oh, it's okay, Daddy," Paula replied. "Mary and Joseph are off on a crusade, and the three wise men are babysitting Jesus."

It stopped Paul in his busy tracks. He did a double take. When he returned to the car where I was waiting, he said, "You won't believe what just happened!" He looked somewhat shaken.

"Are you all right?" I asked, placing my hand on his arm.

"Yeah . . . yeah, I'm okay, but Margie, I have a feeling the Lord has just used our daughter to get our attention." And he told me about the passing conversation.

"When I left her, she added, 'It's okay, Dad. Mary and Joseph are just like you and Mama—they're always gone.'"

I repeated Paula's words: "Mary and Joseph are just like you and Mama—they're always gone. Paul," I said, "that's cute, but it's not funny."

"I know," he replied, glancing sideways at me. His face wore a faraway expression. Once again I guessed that Paul was thinking of his own lonely childhood.

That night, as Paul and I picked up on that conversation again, he commented, "Margie, do you suppose God is telling us to 'be still and know that He is God'?"

We talked about that. One of the emphases in our meetings with parents was to urge them to have time with their kids. Now we had to face the facts: we were too busy ourselves, and it wasn't just because of the ministry. We were getting paid well for what we did, and we had worked out a method whereby churches were actually paying. In the process, however, the girls weren't getting as much as they needed from us.

"Time to practice what we preach," Paul said, and he was so right.

We began scheduling special family nights into our itinerary, when the girls could choose what they wanted to do. We held to it from that point on, and we hold to it even today. We made a promise to God, to each other, and to the children that even though the ministry to children was demanding, it would never push our own daughters out of the center of our love and concern. We believe this is as God would have it, for He Himself established the family as a unit. Never again would our daughters be able to say we were always gone.

In his book, *Too Tough to Cry*, in making reference to this incident in our lives, my husband writes: "God forbid that families should wind up 'castaways' on the barren islands of busyness, or that their children should be abused or neglected. Unfortunately, it happens much too often."

As we came to the close of the 1970s, we wrestled with finding God's will concerning one of the most important decisions we'd ever faced. We felt, for many reasons, that it was time to uproot our family. But it would mean leaving so much behind. There was a tug-of-war going on in our hearts and minds. What were we supposed to do?

***

Reflections on Chapter 13

Your words appeal to audiences of all ages, Margaret. In this chapter, you share some of the choruses you wrote—and we see how very quickly they catch on with everyone. What do you think it is about your writing that gives it such a wide appeal among so diverse a group of individuals?

Quite frankly, I really don't know why my writings have such a broad appeal, other than the fact that I have tried to be honest and open. I also acknowledge the promise of the Holy Spirit dwelling within us to provide insight on behalf of others. Also, there is such a joy and expression in our worship, music writing, and sharing with audiences that I believe it catches on. There is that often-heard expression, "Don't worry, be happy." And I think there is much to be said about its message. A cliché? Perhaps it is. But laughter truly is good for the soul. I think a person receives only what is given to him or to her—nothing more and nothing less.

Part Five—Direction

And let us consider how we may spur one another on toward love and good deeds.

—*Hebrews 10:24*

Chapter 14

MOVING DAY

If the Lord delights in a man's way,
he makes his steps firm.

—*Psalm 37:23*

A new decade. A new life. It was July 1980, and it was moving day.

The moving van was being loaded with our furniture and belongings. Neighbors, family, and friends were sitting on the floor inside the empty house, leaning against the walls, quietly visiting, each dreading the moment of farewell hugs and good-byes. "We've got to run to the lawyer to sign and pick up some documents," Paul said. "Hang tight, everyone, don't go away, we'll be back shortly."

We jumped in our van and drove to the lawyer's office. We signed the final papers for the sale of our home and picked up the six boxes of files that had been at the lawyer's for safekeeping. They included papers that were dear and meaningful to us, including all of the my poems and songs. When we loaded the boxes into our van, which was already practically bulging, the argument began.

"Paul, you know these boxes have got to go with us. They're much too important to load on the moving van."

"No way," he said firmly without even glancing at me. "We have a twenty-five-hundred-mile drive ahead of us—it's a long way to Vancouver, Margie—we need stretching room in this van. You can't load up any more than it already is."

"Oh, but we must!" I countered. "Paul, the things in these boxes are absolutely irreplaceable. What if something happened . . ." My voice trailed off. Paul's face was resolute, and he just drove on, shaking his head.

I had vacillated about moving anyway—one moment excited, the next not overly enthused about going off to British Columbia—and now this. We didn't need a disagreement at this stage—it was all so emotional anyway. One last try. "Paul, my poems are in one of those boxes—all of them, Paul, everything I've ever committed to paper, they're my collections—and there's also our certificates, the blueprints for your magic illusions, awards . . ."

"Trust me, Margie," he said kindly but firmly. "That moving van is loaded with things that are dear and valuable to us. Look, those moving companies are bonded; they have to be trusted. Come on now, lighten up," he added, reaching over to pat my face. A loving gesture, a sweet look on his face as he caught my eye, and I knew I needed to listen to him.

We bounded out of our van and carried the boxes, which were already sealed tightly, over to the moving van. "Just a few more boxes, guys," Paul said. "Looks like you've finished."

"Ready to go!" said the driver.

Paul and I did a quick walk through the house, making certain nothing had been overlooked. Our friends, neighbors, and family members were no longer sitting on the floor; now they all stood around in little clusters. It was time to say good-bye.

All day I'd been fighting back the tears. More than once I'd had to beat a hasty retreat to the bathroom, close and lock the door, and dab at my eyes. Now they overflowed. It didn't help when I looked at the dear familiar faces. Others were crying, too. Good-byes are never easy. We had lived in that house for thirteen years—we had made it a lovely home—and now we were leaving it and all these dear ones behind to go into uncharted territory.

As we pulled away that afternoon, with everyone blowing kisses, waving, and calling out final fare-wells, I had to take charge and remind myself why we were doing this.

The restless feelings had begun some months ear-lier. In fact, it had been in the fall of the previous year that we began to talk to each other about these feelings. "We've been going to the same churches and camps for almost fifteen years, year after year," Paul said. "Perhaps it's time for a change. Besides, the winters here in Ontario are long and cold."

I had to admit he was right. About twice a year—we could count on it—Paul would get walk-ing pneumonia. "And remember all those hous-ing tracts and new churches we saw being built in Vancouver when we were there a year ago? We keep talking about going into full-time ministry. If we're going to do it, we should do so before the girls get any older," I reminded Paul. "Tina will have to switch schools soon anyway."

Back and forth the reasoning went. "Let's put the house up for sale and see what happens. It'll be a sign. Sort of like Gideon's fleece," I said.

But the house didn't sell when we listed it in September, and we shelved the idea of moving. Still, we kept praying, asking God to make His will for our lives very plain.

In conversation with friends at a conference for pastors, Paul learned that British Columbia was considered the new frontier of ministry in Canada. Remembering the enthusiastic reception we'd received when we ministered there, Paul agreed. He came home, and once again the subject came up. "British Columbia is booming!" he exclaimed. "What potential for ministry, Margie!" His eyes sparkled.

Paul and his pastor friends had gotten together at this conference and prayed about this possible move for us and our desire to go into full-time ministry. I had been giving it a lot of thought and prayer, too. I looked up into Paul's dear face and said, "Paul, the potential is there; all we need is the faith."

Once more the house went up for sale—this time in May. And this time, by the end of June, it was sold. Such excitement in the Powers household!

But there was worry too. "How will we support ourselves, Paul?" I asked. "You know it will take time to get a full-time ministry started."

Once again, God orchestrated the events of our lives in such a way that we knew His footprints preceded ours. A job offer from International Audio Visual and Faith Films, a film rental and supply company in Vancouver, paved the way. Paul was hired to do the promotion work for the new Focus on the Family film series, featuring Dr. James Dobson. "And, of course," he was told, "you'll be sales rep for all of the other products we handle." The timing was perfect.

These were my thoughts as our heavily loaded van pulled away. One last glance backward as we left the familiar street and neighborhood. "We're on our way, family," Paul cried out. "All together now," he said. "Vancouver, here we come!"

***

Reflections on Chapter 14

A new decade now begins. You are about to embark on a new life in a new city and fulfill your desire to go into full-time ministry. No doubt it takes motivation and a sense of adventure to make such an important change. Would you say these are two qualities that you possess?

No! I was definitely a homebody and quite terrified to go to the big city when I was married. I loved the security of my family, relatives, friends, and church. I had a strong need to have a career through which I could make a positive difference in my community. I believed I should bloom where I was planted. My experience with something as adventurous as zip-lining came much later in life, when I was enjoying my time with my grandchildren (and not properly prepared and careful as I would normally be). I had too many things on my mind at the time. One must clear all thoughts and distractions when spending time with grandchildren.

Chapter 15

MISSING! GONE! LOST!

When things go wrong, as they sometimes will,
When the road you're trudging seems all up
hill . . .
Stick to the fight when you're hardest hit,
It's when things seem worst that you must
not quit.

—Edgar A. Guest

We were lounging around the pool at the world-renowned Banff Springs Hotel in beautiful Alberta. It was a much-needed treat we were giving ourselves before settling in to the work that awaited us in Vancouver. Tina's school chum was working at the hotel for the summer, so we had an added excuse to spend the weekend there.

We relaxed completely, the long trip from eastern Canada behind us.

After Banff, we went to Lake Louise, where we met Cliff and Billie Barrows. Cliff was one of the Billy Graham team members, and a dear Christian brother.

On the road again, I voiced my concern once more about the cartons we'd put in the moving van at the last minute. "You know everything's going to have to come off the van and go into storage for a month, Paul," I said. "I sure hope we don't lose anything."

"Margie, have you been fretting about that all across the country?"

"Well, yes, I'm afraid so," I responded. "'Oh, ye of little faith,' right?" I tried to sound upbeat.

Paul reached over and patted me. "It's not that you're lacking in faith, Margie; you're human, and your concerns are real. God understands about our humanness. But let's finish out this relaxation interlude by having a good time, okay?"

I nodded in agreement.

Soon the blissful, all-too-brief holiday was over. We arrived in Vancouver the first week of August and found a place to stay for the month, until we could move into a home we hoped to purchase on the first of September. However, that house was sold to someone else, and we were delayed in getting another home.

And then moving-in day arrived! Everything was accounted for, the movers claimed. I walked from room to room looking at the boxes. Noticing my concern, one of the men said, "It's all here, ma'am," as he wiped the perspiration from his brow. Paul signed the papers and the movers left.

Surrounded by cartons and furniture, we began unpacking, setting things in place. But where were the boxes we'd put in the van at the last moment?

"You'll run across them, Margie," Paul reassured me. "Just keep going."

And so I kept going.

So did Paul and the girls. Happy shouts from Tina and Paula let us know they were finding their favorite things.

"Oh . . . look at this lamp," I groaned as I discovered it was broken. When it came to unpacking the china, there were more disappointments and groans. Moving carries with it a certain amount of risk, of course, and we were finding out what that was all about.

By the next day, when most of the boxes had been shifted to appropriate rooms and many had been unpacked, the six cartons from the lawyer's office had still not been found. We checked and double checked.

"Paul, they aren't here. They're missing. Let's face it, they're gone," I said.

Then Paul began berating himself. "Margie, I'm so sorry. I should have listened to you. Just as soon as the phone is connected, I'll notify the movers. They'll find them." He was trying to reassure himself as much as me. "Just remember, your poems are registered with our Toronto lawyer, so if they don't show up, we'll contact him."

Week after week, the calls were made to the moving company. Months passed. My frustration grew. Over and over we were told, "We're searching for your boxes; they're bound to show up somewhere."

I had planned to spend time after the move putting my poems together for publication. Now I had nothing to work with. I alternated between being angry and being totally frustrated. When I sat down to compose, nothing came. It was a devastating loss to me. Paul felt my pain and was sorry about this as well, but it was difficult for him to fully comprehend what I was feeling, even though he had lost things that were important to him, too. Besides, he was busy with his new work and on the road much of the time. His was a big responsibility.

By the end of that first year in Vancouver, the moving company was out of business. By 1982, we still hadn't been able to track down the lost cartons. Then we learned that the company had started up again in Toronto. More phone calls. Finally we discovered the company had declared bankruptcy. We were at a dead end.

"God had His reasons for allowing this loss, Paul," I said as I sought to put meaning to what had happened. "Let's get on with our lives." And that's what we did.

***

Reflections on Chapter 15

There are different losses that we all experience. For you, the loss of your poetry collection—your life's work—must have been positively devastating. Yet you conclude the chapter by saying that God has His reasons. You tell Paul, "Let's get on with our lives." What inspires you to have this positive outlook? What keeps you (and can help keep us) from becoming both bitter and negative?

What keeps me from becoming bitter and thinking negatively? Life lessons learned and experienced tell us that we must be positive as much as we possibly can. Otherwise, our entire physical, spiritual, mental, and emotional being will be at risk of collapsing. We need to help one another and try never to be excessively demanding or critical of others. Instead, we must assist others as much as possible, encouraging them to help themselves.

Chapter 16

THE INFRINGERS

Get rid of all bitterness, rage and anger.
—Ephesians 4:31

In 1983, Paul and I took our daughters with us to the Netherlands for the Conference for Itinerant Evangelists, hosted by the Billy Graham Evangelistic Association. On the way back, we flew to Seattle and rented a car at the airport to drive home to Vancouver. On our drive through Washington state, we visited a Christian bookstore, where we received a great shock: one of the items for sale was a plaque, done in calligraphy, of the "Footprints" poem. I was dumbfounded. To say we were shocked is to put it mildly.

We purchased the plaque to compare it with my

poem, which, of course, I had committed to memory and had since written down. We found the plaque to be very, very close to the original wording of my poem. The name and address of the woman purporting to be the author were on the back of the plaque, and I immediately wrote her. Her husband responded, stating that they would never steal anything and that we ought not to harass them.

Harassment? Surely this was not what we were doing. A simple letter of explanation was all I had written. Thus began a period of unbelievable stress.

We went back to that bookstore and found a dozen other poems I had written, all done in calligraphy on plaques. I wrote the woman and her husband again. There was no response. After our repeated letters to this couple were returned to us unopened, we gave up the effort.

Several weeks later, when we were doing some ministry work on Vancouver Island, we came across the poem again in a bookstore in Victoria. This time it was entitled "I Had a Dream," the title I had given to the original version. The plaque was of beautiful quality. As we looked at the other plaques and bookmarks, we saw that my poems were now being published by a major U.S. publishing company.

Upon our return home, we hired a copyright lawyer in Vancouver. We had received the registration numbers of my poem collections from our Toronto lawyer. The Vancouver lawyer reregistered the material, contacted the publisher, and provided them this information.

The publisher successfully skirted the problem by claiming to have a new manager who would be in touch with us. When this person finally responded, it was to notify us that the publishing company wasn't going to do anything about the matter unless it had proof of government registration for the "Footprints" poem itself. Our lawyer had already sent the company the registration numbers of the collections. It was an exercise in futility and only added to our growing frustration.

Wherever we turned, it seemed, we were bumping into the "Footprints" poem in one form or another. If it wasn't on cups, it was on plates. We found it on bookmarks and cards of every size and shape. Plaques, posters, calendars—you name it, there it was.

After a trip to Sebastopol, California, to attend a leadership conference, Paul and I drove to the pier in San Francisco for a break from the meetings. There we saw a man selling large hand-lettered posters, a new version of "Footprints." But this version was a paraphrase of the original, telling how the man had walked with his friend on the beach, and how he had promised to be faithful to him, but his friend had died of AIDS.

We tried talking to the man selling the posters but he became irate. "Everybody uses it, who cares, how do I know it's yours?"

Tears rolled down my face as I saw what a travesty this was of the beach walk Paul and I had experienced and of the conversation that had prompted the writing of "I Had a Dream" in 1964.

Later on that same trip, before leaving for home, we headed south from San Francisco to beautiful Carmel. We wanted to see the famous monastery there. To our shock, there in the bookstore was a picture of the Virgin Mary with a nun, and, in beautiful handwork, the story of "Footprints" from the vantage point of a nun walking with the Virgin Mary. Once again, we left the bookstore, uncontrolled tears flooding from my eyes.

Another time, in another place, we saw a version of the poem with someone walking with a child. It bothered me to realize how much liberty people were taking with something that had been so meaningful to Paul and me. One woman wrote a book, her autobiography, in which she claimed God had given her the poem. She even had it set to music. I wrote her a letter. She did nothing to take the poem off the market; instead, she sent me an autographed copy of the sheet music. Then someone set the poem in a cross-stitch pattern. I wrote to them, too. It made no difference. People were making too much profit off their products. We spent time and money trying to correct the situation, but it was fruitless, like trying to fight a major fire with a handheld fire extinguisher.

More recently, while writing this, I've seen a version on handprints, a takeoff on "Footprints." We can see that something of the sacredness and special meaning of the piece is being lost.

As Paul and I discussed what was happening and prayed about it, we came to see that this was an infringement on something God had entrusted to me. We shared our concern with a doctor friend from Reno, Nevada, who said, "Look, I know a lawyer who has connections with a copyright lawyer in San Francisco. Maybe you need to talk to another lawyer. Perhaps it's time to look into this more extensively and see if there's something you should be doing to stop these infringements."

"Margie, we can't allow this to make us bitter," Paul cautioned. "We know what God says about that."

I had to agree with him. "I'm upset, Paul, not bitter," I assured him. "At least, I don't think I'm bitter. I'm frustrated because I don't know what, if anything, we are to do. How are you supposed to handle a situation like this?" The question hung in the air. It required an answer.

We finally decided to have the San Francisco lawyer proceed with steps to ensure that the poem's copyright, now under my name, was recognized, and that there would be no more infringements.

***

Reflections on Chapter 16

You reveal how, wherever you turned, you discovered the "Footprints" poem in one form or another. How upsetting for you! Something of the sacredness and the special meaning of the piece was being lost. Through prayer, you came to see that this was an infringement of something with which God had entrusted you. You finally decided to ensure that the poem's copyright, which was under your name, was recognized. At the same time, you understood the words of a famous rabbi who said, "If I am not for myself, who will be for me? If I am not for others, what am I? And if not now, when?"

My name needed to be recognized. There have been other writers in my family, and I have always been a writer of poetry and prose. If I do not protect myself and stand up for who I am, who will? Some people have even tried to do this for me, and I have greatly appreciated it over the years. They know me and know my work. At the same time, if I do not care about others, what kind of person am I? And if I don't care about people today, then will I have other opportunities?

This is why I still help in prison ministry, even when people think I am too busy and ask why I should bother. We have to have a very good reason not to be involved. If I can make a difference in even one life, then it is well worth it. And I believe we have made a difference in many lives over the years. This is why we have worked so diligently to teach and train children, so that they will not be incarcerated and lonely in their future adult life. We want to give them some skills, love, and hope for their future—and that desire is derived from the Bible. The words of that rabbi, Rabbi Hillel, certainly reflect my thinking.

Chapter 17

THE PUZZLE

See to it that no one misses the grace of God
and that no bitter root grows up to cause
trouble.

—Hebrews 12:15

My mother and my aunt came to visit us right about the time we were agonizing over what to do about the "Footprints" poem. "It's like putting a giant puzzle together," I recall saying as I explained our dilemma.

In fact, at the time we had an extremely large jigsaw puzzle on the dining-room table that I'd spent hours working on. I pointed to the puzzle as I talked to Mom and my aunt. "How are you doing with it?" Mom asked as she nodded toward the table.

"Well, sometimes it can drive you crazy," I replied, laughing. "Then I get up, go for a walk around the block, or go to work. But I always keep going back!" My mother smiled knowingly.

"One of these days you'll have your answer," she said wisely, and this time she wasn't pointing at the puzzle.

Days later, after they were gone, I proudly exclaimed to the family that the puzzle was done. I had such a sense of satisfaction! It was beautiful. So beautiful, in fact, that Paul and Paula secretly decided they'd put it on a board and have it mounted for the friends who had looked after our home while we were working in Australia and New Zealand. "Won't Mom be surprised!" they said to each other. And so, one day when I was out, they tackled the moving of the puzzle. They tried it very carefully, but suddenly the whole thing fell apart. To say they were absolutely beside themselves would be an understatement. And how would I handle it? That was the big question.

I didn't handle it well. I felt outraged when I came back and discovered what had happened. Although I tried to conceal it, I felt angry for several weeks.

But even worse, I could tell that what I was feeling was bitterness. Gradually, it came to me that I had developed this bitterness in my life over a period of time, but I hadn't been able to admit it. Normally, a situation such as the one with the puzzle wouldn't bother me. I would just laugh and say, "Let's start that puzzle again. This time you're all going to have to help!" and we'd laugh and joke about it.

But that wasn't what had happened. "I don't ever want to see that puzzle again or have anything to do with it," I'd said as I stormed out of the room, crying.

It was our daughter Paula who confronted me lovingly. "Mom, you're bitter. Something's eating away at you. You've got to get rid of it," she said as she opened the Bible. Putting her arm around me, she read from Ephesians 4:30–31 and Hebrews 12:14–15. "Do not grieve the Holy Spirit of God . . . Get rid of all bitterness, rage and anger . . . Make every effort to live in peace with all men and to be holy . . . See to it that . . . no bitter root grows up to cause trouble."

I thanked her for caring so much that she dared to tell me what I needed to hear. We hugged each other and cried together. Paula knew I was hurting deep inside. The episode with the puzzle was symptomatic of what was going on in my heart, and God had given her the wisdom to recognize it and then the courage to talk to me.

Now began some soul-searching. God, what do I do with the guilt that others should have? What is this bitterness that I'm experiencing? This anger? Why am I feeling so strongly about what's happened? I've tried never to let the sun go down on my wrath—I believe in settling matters. Help me, Lord. I need understanding and direction. I'm puzzled.

***

Reflections on Chapter 17

There is often a connection between the tangible and the intangible. In this chapter, it is significant that a broken jigsaw puzzle serves as your metaphor. As you say, the episode of the puzzle and your uncharacteristic reaction to it was symptomatic of what was going on in your heart. Your daughter Paula helped put things in perspective. Soon you began some seri-ous soul-searching, and another broken puzzle would be mended. It's easy for us to lose our perspective. Sometimes small things can throw us off-kilter. Do you have a good "tonic" that helps keep things from mushrooming out of proportion?

Yes, when I see that things are building up or overwhelming me, or if the other person seems confrontational, I ask to be excused and I walk away from the situation. I need time out. Being a teacher, I think this manner of handling explo-sive situations is very wise. I will go on to do some housekeeping or laundry (I have always been a multitasker; I think my grandmother and mother invented the word!), or I put in half-a-dozen jigsaw puzzle pieces. Then I take a long walk until I am ready to calmly face the problem again. That's when I miss having a dog to walk!

I never like to say hurtful words that will forever inflict pain on the other person, and I don't wish to have the other person embarrass or humiliate himself or herself to the point of no recovery. My father instilled in me this "life's little lesson," as he felt that many people could easily make a disagreement evaporate if they just listened, used little words, were never loose-lipped, and took time and patience to work out the problem. Each person looks at a situation with a different viewpoint.

We were never allowed to grumble, sing, or hum during mealtimes, and we learned to keep our aches and pains to ourselves unless we needed to confide in our mother about a medical condition of any importance. To help us relax and enjoy ourselves, our home always had jigsaw or crossword puzzles for people to work on during their spare time and to pass on to the next member of the family to do at their leisure. Even our little dog Patti would sit and watch us play games or put puzzles together. It was relaxing, fun, and often a fruitful fellowship time.

My eldest daughter puts on a cup of tea to have with a homemade treat, and problems seem to melt away. My British friend, Beryl, puts out a "cuppa" and shortbread cookies whenever we are all tired or need a break or the minute her grandchildren arrive. The problems just seem to disappear. In her living room is a handmade "seal of approval," a gift from a young guest grateful for her hospitality, for being the best hostess in the world. It isn't the food, I suppose, but the kindness and gentleness and sincerity of love that seep into the day.

My friends in Wales, Pam and Barry and Victoria, serve shortbread cookies and scones with clotted cream. Everyone in the room "melts and gains weight." These are just some of the tonics we use to cope with life's little challenges.

My friend Dame Thora would tell me that I would be happy if I just kept my front and back home entrance clean and ready for guests to enter. Much could be said about that advice even today, whether we have a tiny tent, a trailer, a mud hut, or an elegant castle to call home.

I'm so thankful that my sisters and my daughters share these values. It is lovely to hear compliments from their friends and families who enjoy their friendship and hospitality. My sister's door always has a welcome mat and a wreath.

We were taught to do our tasks first, without grumbling or complaining, and with a smile that didn't take effort. We were reminded to say kind things to each other every day, and to be sincere about it. We had our own chores, which gave us a sense of personal worth and value. I recently observed my youngest granddaughter doing some shredding for me. In no uncertain terms she told her brother that this was her "job," and he shouldn't interfere with her special task. I suddenly saw myself in her.

Chapter 18

RELINQUISHMENT

I sought the Lord, and he answered me.

—*Psalm 34:4*

There was no audible voice, but God answered my cry for help.

I began to realize how difficult it had been for Paul to live with my frustration and pain for so many years. Even though our Little People's Ministry had taken hold and was growing, and we experienced the blessings of God in our lives, still, in my heart, I carried a sense of profound loss about the poems— my life's work. After the conversation with Paula, it was as if God were unscrolling a part of my life that I'd kept hidden: "Bitterness, my child, is related to the people who are closest to you. They are the ones who feel the fallout from your emotions, your anger, and your frustration.

Your own daughter Tina, for instance, hasn't wanted anyone to know that you wrote the 'Footprints' poem, or many others that she has seen in print. She's been very cautious not to let her friends at college know. Why, Margie, why? Bitterness hurts a lot of people. Your precious daughter is hurting because you are hurting. She doesn't fully understand her feelings; they are troubling to her, but it's what's happened to the poems that's hurting you, and so she doesn't want to admit that the poem is yours.

"Bitterness is often based upon what someone has done to you. It may also have its roots in somebody else's sin, if you know about it and you feel they are getting away with something. But don't you know, Margie, that there is nothing hidden from Me? You've had a heavy burden on your heart for a long time. You've felt that you were being sinned against. I see your tender conscience. You do have a problem, however, and you need to let it go.

"You haven't wanted to be rid of your dilemma. You've become accustomed to it.

"Yes, I know, at times you feel things are going along just fine and you experience peace, but habits become binding, and they can strangle your personality. You are no longer the lighthearted girl Paul married. Like a lot of bitter people, you are bitter over something that happened many years ago.

"Every time you go into a Christian bookstore you are confronted with your feelings. Try as you will to submerge them, they keep popping up to remind you. There is visible evidence in these stores to disturb you—you see evidence of 'Footprints' everywhere you turn. You love these bookstores— some of the happiest years of your marriage were spent when you and Paul both worked in one in Toronto. Are you going to continue to allow these feelings to fester?

"Margie, for seven years you've lived with this. You've done your best to write to people and to companies to explain the loss and the ownership of the poem. You've received many responses concerning it, but no one is willing to stop using the poem or publishing it, because it's making them a lot of money.

"You've had one lawyer tell you to allow this to

continue because it could work as a tremendous asset in your favor—a better reason for a lawsuit.

"Dear child, I can see that you don't want this bitterness to keep springing up to cause you trouble. You do understand what I mean. You and Paul aren't mercenary—money isn't the object, it's not the reason for your feelings. I see into your heart. Here . . . here is peace of mind. Take it, Margie. Forgive and forget. Let Me handle it. Let Me carry it for you."

No, I repeat, this was not audible but spoken to my troubled heart. I knew what had to be done. I had to relinquish the pain, the right to feel angry, I had to let it go. All of it. It was stubborn, like a plant with roots that went down deep. If I was to experience that special grace of God and the peace of mind He promises to those who obey His Word and trust Him, then it was indisputably necessary for Margie Powers to take her hands off the reins of her life, to forgive and to forget.

By this time, there were two Canadian lawyers and two American copyright lawyers anxious to take up the case. Relinquishment would not come easy. Could I do it?

***

Reflections on Chapter 18

This chapter is entitled "Relinquishment," and from the readers' letters that appear later in the book in the section "Letters and Recollections," I see that many people have identified with its message. In this chapter, you still carry a sense of loss about the poems and need to make an important decision. Do you finally rid yourself of the bitterness you have been carrying? Is it time to forgive and forget and let God carry the burden for you?

Yes, I have had to rid myself of any bitterness and worry that has plagued me in the past. Forgiveness is clearing the conscience! A clear conscience makes a softer pillow to sleep on at night. The difficult thing is to try to forget, so you have to just give your burden over to the Lord. He is the one who can sustain us over a long period. Letting God carry the burden. I remember a thought by one of my advisers:

You can stop forgiving others who have done you a great injustice only if you are ready for Christ to stop forgiving you. That thought made an impact on my thinking. One of my favorite verses during high school was Philippians 3:13: "Forgetting what is behind and straining toward what is ahead."

Chapter 19

"Leave It There"

Just leave it with the Lord,
The One you most adore,
He will bless and give sweet rest,
Just leave it with the Lord.

Thank God for the wonderful others He places in our lives.

"Mother, what do you think we should do?" I was making a long-distance call to my mom on November 25, 1987. She knew that we had to give the lawyers the green light to go ahead with a lawsuit or put a stop to the whole thing.

"Well, now, what would your father advise you? What would he have thought, Margie?" Dad had passed away ten years before, but we still thought of his good sense when we faced difficult decisions.

Of course, I knew what his answer would be—that he would not have wanted me to take up a lawsuit against anyone—and I told my mother so.

"You still have to make the decision, my dear," she said.

"Now they're saying we have to prove that the poem is mine, come up with an original copy of the poem. You know I can't provide that."

There was a pause. "Just a moment," she said, and I could tell she was thinking some more. "Your wedding book . . . what about your wedding material?"

"What do you mean, my 'wedding material'?"

"I'm sure you wrote some of those poems in your wedding album before you and Paul were married."

"Mother!" I gasped. "I did. Yes, I know I did."

It was as if the last piece of the puzzle had been found. I dropped the phone, ran to where I kept the wedding album, and there it was! "Mother, Mother, you're right! I've found it. Yes, I wrote it in our wedding book. It's here . . . it's here!" I was jumping and shouting into the phone at the same time.

Both Paul and I had forgotten about the album. We hadn't looked at it in years. Our lives were busy, the Little People's Ministry kept us on the move, we were parents with girls who understandably required a lot of our time and attention. Mother's words were as though just the right door had opened.

That was also the day when we discussed the decision that faced us with our dear friend "Uncle" Geoffrey Still, Canadian representative of Focus on the Family. "Go home, Margie," he said, "and write a three-verse piece for me, and I think you'll find great release and freedom about this situation."

"Uncle Geoff"—I fumbled for the right words to tell him—"I haven't been able to write for a long time. It's like . . ." I paused, fumbling again.

"Go on," he encouraged me. "Like what?"

"Well, I facetiously call it 'The Great Brain Robbery,' but I just haven't been writing. And now we've actually found an original inside our wedding album. Does this mean we have the green light from God to continue? Oh, I'm so confused."

"She's right," Paul chimed in. "It's disturbed me for quite some time. Margie seems to have lost the enjoyment in writing that she used to have. She doesn't even write songs anymore. And the fact that we've found an original copy in our wedding album—well, it does seem to cloud the issue. Actually, I thought we'd pretty much made up our minds to drop the lawsuit. Now this. I'm confused, too."

"I don't think I'll ever be able to write again," I said sadly.

"No, no, that's not true," Uncle Geoff reassured me.

"I wouldn't even know where to start if I did as you've suggested and tried to put my feelings in words on paper."

"Margie and Paul, it's time to put this whole matter into perspective. You need to answer this question: Will it have a negative effect on innocent people if you decide to pursue legal action? What about your ministry? Our choices always affect others. It's like throwing a pebble in a pond; there's a ripple effect. God has blessed the use of that poem worldwide. Will that be hindered? The most important consideration is: What does God require? What does the Bible say about such matters?"

Uncle Geoffrey was articulating what we'd discussed, but just hearing him say it did, indeed, put it in perspective.

"Margie," Uncle Geoff asked, "can you just leave it with the Lord?" The three of us looked at each other, the same thought dawning on us. "That's it," he said. "Go home, write your heart out, and call it 'Leave It There.'"

And that's what I did. In the early hours of the morning I was awakened, and an entire song with words and music came to me. I picked up my little flashlight on the nightstand, the pen, and the notepad, and scribbled out the words to three verses. I didn't even get out of bed. When I was finished, I was so tired, I fell right back to sleep.

That morning, upon arising, I remembered the incident. I carried the notepad with me to the kitchen table. It was like hieroglyphics. When I finally figured it out, after working at it until almost noon, I had the musical score in my head, as well as the words. And Uncle Geoff was right—writing did help me to sort out my feelings. I remembered the conversation I felt had taken place between God and me; I thought about my mother's words; I

176

knew what my father would have said; I knew what the Bible said about taking Christian brothers to court; and I already knew how Paul felt. It was the right decision—I would leave it all with God.

Leave It There

Just leave it with the Lord,
The One you most adore,
He will bless and give sweet rest,
Just leave it with the Lord.
Just place it at His feet,
You know that He'll complete,
The work you've done has just begun,
Place your burden at His feet.
O Lord, I do delight in You,
And on Your care depend,
And know that as my trouble flees
You'll always be my Friend.

The words were based on 1 Peter 5:7—"Cast all your anxiety on him because he cares for you."

The decision was made. There would be no lawsuit.

Reflections on Chapter 19

You express your gratitude for the wonderful people God places in our lives, beginning with your mother. Your mother has a thought about the lost "Footprints," and "it was as if the last piece of the puzzle had been found." At last you are able to write again, a beautiful poem called "Leave It There." Your mother must have been a very practical person to realize that the last piece of the puzzle was in fact so close. There's a theory that when we misplace something—our keys, for instance—it's generally within a mere three feet or so of where it should be. Do you feel that the answers to our questions—to what we are searching for—are sometimes much closer than we realize?

My mom was definitely a practical person, and she seemed to have the ability to delve into her storehouse of wisdom to help her solve the many problems that came with being a daughter, a wife, and the mother of six children. Today we would say she was a master at multitasking. She was not perfect, but she loved and cared for each of her kids.

I think the real measure of the treasure that my mother was is what was in her heart. She seldom lost her temper, and I remember her crying only three times in my life. Mostly, I remember how painful that was for my father. I think she was a very strong woman (although not particularly strong physically). Today, I still treasure all of her cards and handwritten letters, which can be found in her fancy flowered box. I love the description of the future King David from Samuel 16:7—"Man looks at the outward appearance, but the Lord looks at the heart." My mother's Scripture study helped her to raise a large family and still take part in her church and community. (Readers may enjoy my tribute to my mom, found later in the book in the section "Letters and Recollections.")

I am pleased to tell you that since I made the decision not to sue, a number of individuals and companies in North America have signed publishing contracts through HarperCollins Publishers and the San Francisco lawyers, and people in other countries are in final discussions concerning contracts for the use of "Footprints" memorabilia.

Part Six—Peace

Whatever you have learned or received or heard from me, or seen in me—put it into practice. And the God of peace will be with you.

—*Philippians 4:9*

Chapter 20

THE PEACE OF GOD

Make every effort to live in peace with all men.
—Hebrews 12:14

Everyone—Paul, our daughters, my mother, Geoffrey Still, and friends with whom we shared our decision—was relieved to learn we had decided against legal action. It was Geoffrey Still who suggested we write a letter to those whom we had contacted about the use of the poem. The letter was written and dated November 30, 1987:

Pursuant to my letter of [date], I want to make one final plea. I have been in touch with Mr.———, a copyright lawyer in San Francisco. His direction was to pursue legal action in order to protect my authorship of "I Had a Dream" and the various versions of that poem now distributed as "Footprints."

As a Christian I have chosen not to take legal action. However, I once again request that all future printings of the poem "Footprints" show my authorship.

I wrote the poem October 10, 1964. The original manuscript was lost in a move from Toronto to Vancouver. "I Had a Dream" was republished in "Heart to Heart," a poetry collection under my name, in 1985 in Hamilton, Bermuda [and which I had started to negotiate the publication of in February 1980]. Just recently, an original copy of the poem was discovered.

That year, Hallmark asked for rights to use "Footprints" and the poem "Letter from a Friend" in its cards. Several other companies, including firms in Germany and Japan, have use of the poems as well.

Today I can walk into any bookstore and feel comfortable about the decision that was made. I am no longer bitter that others have used my work, even though I don't like some of the adaptations they have made for their own purposes. I have learned to forgive and forget as the Lord has gently nudged me along to more important things. And in setting aside my feelings of ownership to these words that God put into my heart, I have at last escaped the frustrations that were making my life—and my family's life—so difficult. I feel I have recovered my wholeness of heart. That's what the peace of God does for you.

The trials that we have had—Paula's terrible fall at Golden Ears Park and Paul's heart attack—have reminded me that we must save our strength and will to live our lives to God's purposes and not fritter them away on personal grievances. My family and I are at peace again, after difficult times. Our work with children, the citizens of tomorrow, continues unhindered.

I am deeply moved when I hear accounts of what the poem "Footprints" has meant to someone. Following the 1990–91 Persian Gulf crisis, for instance, I read a newspaper account of Lance-Corporal Mark Schrader, a young, self-effacing Marine from Tennessee who risked his life in an Iraqi minefield. He miraculously survived. The next morning, the crews in their tankers studied the terrain and found seven mines and some trip-wires alongside his footprints. They told him he was either the stupidest or the luckiest Marine alive.

Lance-Corporal Mark Schrader told his buddies, and later the media, "I didn't see any trip-wires!" Afterward, squad members talked about the incident and someone mentioned the poem "Footprints." "It was obviously not my footprints that went through that minefield," the young hero maintains. "It was God. He carried me."

That story alone has made it all worthwhile.

It is my earnest prayer that the true story of "I Had a Dream" and the title by which it is most known, "Footprints," will have an even more God-blessed ministry in the days to come, as the reader sees how this very human writer struggled with her feelings, but how God lovingly carried her. What God has done for me, what He did for the young Marine, God will do for anyone who asks Him to walk with them through life.

***

Reflections on Chapter 20

In this chapter you write that, in setting aside your feelings of ownership to the words that God put into your heart, you at last escaped the frustrations that were making your life—and your family's life—so difficult. You felt you recovered your wholeness of heart. That's what the peace of God did for you. Can you share a few more thoughts on the words "peace of God" and how we can achieve it?

Peace is a very fragile thing. A number of passages from Scripture bring me comfort. In Psalm 31:15, King David begins to find peace when he acknowledges to the Lord, "My times are in your hands." The trust that he places in God—that is peace. I also find myself turning to Isaiah 26:3–4: "You will keep in perfect peace him whose mind is steadfast, because he trusts in you. Trust in the Lord forever." In my own situation, there was a time when I felt nervous and afraid for my husband's life and health, and

I didn't want to share that deep concern with anyone. Then my longtime friend and pastor, Stan Starkey, urged me to face the issues, to let God know I was afraid and couldn't face being alone without my wonderful life partner and friend. I did that—and was blessed with a sense of peace.

Chapter 21

STEP BY STEP

How great is the love the Father has lavished
on us . . .

—1 John 3:1

Our daughter Paula's sixty-eight-foot fall from
the top of the glacier waterfalls in August of
1989 ushered in a time of sorrow and devastation
for our family. A month after the accident, doctors at Maple Ridge General and Royal Columbian
Hospitals informed us that our daughter would live
and would walk again, but that her recovery would
be slow and tedious. Some of her injuries were per-
manent. Additional tests and visits with specialists
revealed that Paula would not be able to have children and that the nerves in her right arm and hand

could not be repaired. For the foreseeable future, she would need care around the clock.

As her situation improved, however, Paula became anxious to reclaim her life. Dr. Thomas and Sue Standlee, medical family friends from Reno, Nevada, offered to help Paula continue her university education, freeing Paul and me to carry on with Little People's Ministry. Paula moved to Reno after Christmas and began her course in education at University of Nevada, Reno—UNR for short—in January of 1991.

Wonderful things began to happen for Paula there. In March she met UNR student Thomas Callahan, who was attending the same prayer group and Bible study groups. By the time we met Tom that summer, Paula had told us quite a lot about him in her letters, and we hit it off wonderfully well. In 1993, Tom moved to Montreal to attend McGill University. That winter, he came to visit us in Vancouver and discuss his future with Paula.

Tom's intentions toward Paula were formalized in the summer of 1995, when he came to Vancouver to be part of Little People's Team Vacation Bible School ministry. Late one afternoon at the park across from our home, Tom proposed to Paula and presented her with a beautiful diamond ring. The sparkle in her eyes as she described the event to us later was even more dazzling than the stone.

Many hours of discussion followed concerning the state of Paula's health and Tom and Paula's future—without children. Of greatest urgency were the medical tests and paperwork required by U.S. Immigration in order for Paula and Tom to marry and live in the United States.

The wedding date was set for June 8, 1996, in Reno. The final immigration paper arrived on May 30, and the next day we loaded the moving van and headed that way. We arrived on June 2 and rented an apartment to prepare for the big event.

The wedding, held at the First Evangelical Free Church of Reno, Nevada, was all that we dreamed it would be. The bride was beautiful in her white satin gown with Ancient Barclay tartan sash. (Barclay is her father's Scottish clan.) Even though the young couple faced an uncertain future, it was truly a glorious moment in time.

But a year and a half later, a serious problem had to be dealt with. For almost a year before her wedding,

Paula had been experiencing terrible headaches and trouble with her eyesight. At times she would see black spots and then there would be an interruption in her vision. By 1998, the problem had become so severe that she was virtually blind. Her ophthalmologist suggested an operation to relieve the pressure on her brain. Even though there was little promise of success, Paula decided to move ahead with it, willing to try anything that might restore even a portion of her eyesight. The surgery was scheduled for January 13, 1998.

A month earlier, Paul had suffered several mild heart attacks, and his doctor had scheduled him for a heart bypass. However, we decided to let Paul's situation ride for a short time so that we could be in Reno for Paula's eye surgery. On January 9, I called my mother to inform her of Paul's situation and ask for her prayers. Our brief chat, filled with discussion of the Christmas just past, family, and prayer, would be our last. Mom died later that day.

After the funeral in Toronto, we arrived back in Reno the night before Paula's operation, and we were up and ready to go early the next morning. Even though there was little reason to hope, we possessed a calm assurance of God's presence.

Later that day, we were told that Paula's surgery had gone well. The final outcome would not be known, however, until the eyes had healed enough for the bandages to be removed. Only then would we know for sure.

Tom kept a close vigil over his wife, especially after she was released from the hospital. The four of us stayed together in their Reno apartment, waiting and praying. When the bandages were finally removed, we were delighted with the result. By the time we left for Canada, Paula's recovery was coming along nicely.

During our stay in Reno caring for our daughter, the situation with Paul's heart worsened. A short time after we returned home in February, he suffered two more heart attacks and had a triple bypass. The night before the surgery, Paul felt the Lord leading him to a particular Scripture—Genesis 28:15. Early the next morning, our pastor came to the hospital to pray with Paul and read him the exact same passage: "I am with you and will watch over you wherever you go, and I will bring you back to this land. I will not leave you until I have done what I have promised you." It was no surprise to us that God kept His word. Paul's surgery was a success.

A few years later, Tom and Paula moved from Reno to Pocatello, Idaho. Paula, her eyesight now stabilized, drove back and forth to Reno in order to finish her degree in education. She graduated in June of 1999.

In September, during one of our visits, we received wonderful news that could only be described as miraculous. A phone call from her doctor confirmed that Paula was pregnant. We were all excited despite the doctor's warning that there was a strong possibility of a miscarriage. More medical updates would come after we got back from our ministry trip to Europe. It was difficult to leave and even more difficult to keep my mind on ministry. Every newborn we saw brought new anxiety about Paula and her health.

Paula's fragile pregnancy survived with God's tender care. The doctors monitored her twice a week and set a due date for late April. But on February 25, while we were attending a home missions prayer meeting, Tom called to announce that Paula had been taken to the hospital. The next morning, after a sleepless, prayer-filled night, Tom called again, this time to confirm that a miracle had taken place. A child—Calvin Arthur Callahan—had been born almost two months premature. Our delicate little grandson, otherwise completely healthy, weighed in at only two pounds. On March 6, the day we arrived to help out, Paula and Calvin came home from the hospital. Though the baby was still tiny, he, along with his mother, was well on his way to recovery.

God's blessings on the entire family continued when, on December 10, 2003, Corinna Margaret Callahan arrived three weeks early. God has blessed Tom and Paula with two miracles—two beautiful babies to keep us mindful of His grace and goodness.

***

Time plays funny tricks on us. Something that seems to have happened yesterday, so clear and precise, is actually an event that took place over forty-five years ago. Often I think twice about things that happened just a few days ago.

In the investments of our life, we reflect on

"cost" and "value." I must admit there were some decisions we made that we lost out on emotionally, physically, and financially. But perhaps those choices had a spiritual worth we could not appreciate. I continue to invest in things that are of great personal and spiritual value in my life.

My husband and I have frequently reminded ourselves and our children of the great value God has placed on us when we see the price of purchase on the Cross by His Son (1 Timothy 2:5–6). We have observed many life investments that still pay dividends and will continue to do so, to us and to many others. For example, we have witnessed an outpouring of support for youth in the United Kingdom and elsewhere. We have seen an increasing number of young men become pastors in several Caribbean islands. We have been observers as babies are cared for in orphanages throughout Latin America, and we have seen improvements in survival rates, methods of care, and accommodation in places that don't benefit from the tourist trade and where income is therefore painfully small.

Now we are preparing to invest in our grandchildren. When we can, we will give advice, love, encouragement, and support for their physical and spiritual needs. What a great privilege it is to be called on when we can help. What a great privilege it is to be called "friend."

I wish I could recall each story I have heard about those whose lives have been lifted up by the words of my poem "I Had a Dream"—or "Footprints in the Sand." I have found that its words are not limited to one age group, culture, or spiritual persuasion, and it is a blessing that the poem has brought comfort to people of diverse cultures and walks of life. The following section of the book includes some responses from people who were kind enough to share their thoughts.

***

Reflections on Chapter 21

In this chapter, the story comes full circle. We look forward to hearing about the next chapters of your life. Before we say goodbye, would you like to reflect on some of the fascinating, sometimes challenging, events you have shared with us?

After reflecting at length on the impact of the events of my life, I recognize that they will be part of the legacy I leave my children, grandchildren, and great-grandchildren. I hope the collective aspects of my life's story will show God's great faithfulness, demonstrated in miraculous ways throughout the years of my life. My mother's favourite hymn was "Great Is Thy Faithfulness," the wonderful song. It is my favourite as well. I look ahead with much anticipation to the future and want to walk step by step and day by day in unison with God.

Just today, my eight-year-old granddaughter placed her first puzzle piece into a difficult adult-level jigsaw. What a delight for her! There are still many pieces of the puzzle of my life to be put into place. And it encourages me to gaze far into the future—with hope, inspiration, and dreams. My daughter has always had a picture on her wall of a white Scottie dog standing sturdily on a high pile of suitcases. With the wind at its back, the little dog stares intently out to the rolling sea. That picture reminds me of a great adventure yet to be. I don't want to miss a minute of it!

Letters and Recollections

Dear Margaret Fishback Powers:

I would love to share with you how your book and poem have touched and inspired me.

I was sitting at my piano playing a song that I had composed previously called "Going Home." I finished the piece and continued playing some other chords. Before I knew it, I was playing a melody I had never heard before. It was just flowing out of me, so to speak. I was in total awe.

Your poem came to mind while I was wondering what words could be used with this new melody. I ran to the bedroom and grabbed my copy of your book, *Footprints: The True Story Behind the Poem That Inspired Millions.*

I started playing the tune again, and it went exactly with your words. I was shocked that this had happened and I looked up to the ceiling and said, "Why me, Lord?" And a quiet calm voice said, "Why not?"

I can tell you that since that day I have been walking a different path that I never guessed I would take. The music to "Footprints" is calling me to do more with my life.

With your blessing, I now look forward to producing my CD and video—adding more dimension to my music ministry.

Yours in Christ,
Melissa
Texas

*

Dear Mrs. Powers:

You have undoubtedly heard thousands of stories about how your poem has comforted and inspired families and individuals around the world. This is one more of those stories, which isn't finished yet.

Several Sundays ago, the minister in our little country church in Muskoka told us the story behind "Footprints" during our children's time. A week or so later (Dec 7th) my wife, Linda, was diagnosed with a brain tumor, which will require surgery in Toronto on January 9. They believe it is benign but one can't help going through all the worst scenarios—especially at 3 a.m. Your poem came back to our minds immediately, and we found it comforting. Days later, the mail brought us three bookmarks with your poem (correctly attributed, by the way!). Your poem just kept coming and coming to us.

God works in interesting ways because I had no idea how to get in touch with you until a Mississauga friend and his local Christian bookstore owner knew someone who knew you. It was your brother James who very kindly gave me your address over the phone this morning. I have much more to say, but I'll close this by saying that I have been reading whole sections of your book to my wife, Linda, and it has been a great comfort to us at this time in our lives.

God Bless,
Jack
Ontario

*

Dear Margaret:

One of my sons gave me your book, *Footprints*, as a Christmas present. He couldn't have chosen a better gift. Both my wife and I have read it with great interest, for the poem has a special place in our memories.

Five years ago I was stricken with a virus that collapsed my lungs and punctured them both in seven or eight places. This resulted in me spending one month in intensive care, two months in the general ward at the hospital, and a year at home on oxygen.

I am not fully recovered, but my blood now has the

capacity to make oxygen at 80 percent efficiency, so I operate reasonably well. When I came out of intensive care and was lying in my private room, I had a visit from the surgeon who had operated on me a few times. This fellow may well have been a fine surgeon, but he was totally lacking in human skills. I still remember one operation that he did while I was partially conscious and scared. He told me, standing in the doorway, that if the leaks in my lungs didn't heal themselves within two months, he would have to operate again. My specialist and GP hadn't told me about this, as they were concentrating on building a positive attitude to help the healing process. I was frightened and did not know how I could handle the situation—and then I remembered a poem that a friend had given me that very afternoon. It was your poem. I read it again and the answer came to me. I then talked to God and told him that because I was incapable of worrying about future operations and building a positive attitude at the same time, I would leave the future to him and would concentrate instead on being positive each day. Having had this talk and made this decision, I relaxed, for I knew that he would carry me.

Two months later, the surgeon appeared again and commented on the fact that I still had one leak in a lung that had not healed. He said that he would therefore have to operate the following week! That night I talked to God and pointed out that he had done a fine job of healing, but that he now would have to go into high gear or my worst fear would come true.

I awakened the next morning as usual, while the nurse was inspecting the bottle containing the fluids still leaking from my lung. In fact, I awoke rather quickly because she said, "It's stopped leaking!" I couldn't believe it and neither could she, since the leaks always sealed themselves off gradually over the period of a week or more and this one had just stopped—period. When the specialist came in later that day, he examined the drainage bottle and said that there must be a blockage somewhere, and left instructions for a resident doctor to inspect the attachment to my body. Result? Nothing wrong! After a week of waiting, the doctors decided that "for some reason" the leak had healed itself and I could go home, without any further surgery!

I have since had a friend write your poem in calligraphy, and have given framed copies to all my children. Of course, I have the original on the wall of our guest bedroom.

Thank you, Margaret, for writing that poem. It has certainly been a great comfort to me. I have now inscribed your name on the back of the framed copy.

Paul
Alberta

*

Dear Mrs. Powers:

I have, in the past five minutes, finished reading your book concerning the history of "I Had a Dream," or "Footprints." I could not put your book down after I picked it up, and read it in just over two hours. These past two hours have been another trip to the mountaintop of Peace.

I would like to relate to you my experience with the

beautiful poem that God entrusted to you. I was on transfer from National Defence headquarters to the naval base at Esquimalt. During the drive out west I visited with my sister near Edmonton. On her dining-room wall hung a copy of your poem. I was instantly taken by the beauty of its imagery. I asked my sister to mail me a copy of it should she ever find it in another store. I was not a practicing Christian at this time but I had been raised with a Christian background. I stopped going to church about the same time you wrote this work.

After arriving in Esquimalt, a package arrived from my sister with my first copy of "Footprints" in it. I took great pleasure in hanging it in my dining room and read it daily. A few weeks after I hung it over my dining-room table, a close friend experienced the tragic loss of his wife due to an aneurysm in her brain. My friend was devastated and began a grieving process that made him drink very heavily. One night he wrecked his car and almost killed himself in the process. I, along with the rest of his friends, was becoming very concerned for his safety. One evening as I ate my evening meal, I looked at "Footprints" and the answer came to me. I took "Footprints" down and walked over to my friend's house, not sure what I was going to say or if I'd still have this friend when I returned home. I went into his kitchen and told him to sit down and listen to me. I voiced my concerns for him, and then gave him the copy of "Footprints" and left. That was ten years ago. My friend is remarried and very happy. Above his bed hangs my first copy of "Footprints."

It would be enough if the story ended there, but that was only the beginning. As you are well aware, God moves in mysterious and wonderful ways. "Footprints" was the beginning of a personal spiritual odyssey that led me to a new career. This September I begin studies and with the grace of God will be ordained to holy orders in about three years' time. The road I have traveled to come this far has been scattered with obstacles and periods of deep questioning. Through it all, when times looked the bleakest, "Footprints" has reminded me of the support and love that God gives us so freely. And now thanks to your wonderful work, I have another reminder to look toward when times get tough: "Leave It There."

I was moved to tears reading this, especially since I am trying to deal with an obstacle that could prevent me from attending school in the fall. "Leave It There" has helped to remove this burden.

Your Servant in Christ,
Sandy
Saskatchewan

*

Dear Margaret:

In May of 1987, God saw fit to take home our four-month-old baby son. It was during that time a very close friend of mine sent me the reading "Footprints." "Footprints" became my confirmation that God would not leave me when I so desperately needed Him. My husband and I read that little poem literally hundreds of times, as a reminder to us that God's mighty hand was at work. We believed that God would somehow mend our broken hearts, dry our falling tears, and rebuild our lives so that we could continue to serve Him. My special thanks to

you, Margie, for allowing God to inspire these
precious words in your heart.

Love in Christ,
Kelvin and Leah
New Brunswick

*

Dear Mrs. Powers:

I read your book *Footprints* this evening and am
inspired to write to you and tell you how very much
your beautiful poem has meant to me.

In 1969 or 1970 I was about twelve or thirteen years
old and did not yet know the Lord. I was, however,
about to enter a crisis in my life that would last the
rest of my teen years. One night back then, I really
did "have a dream" whereby the Lord revealed to
me that my mother was having an affair. I did not
know it was the Lord at the time who revealed this
to me, and all I ever remembered of the dream was a
horrible sinking feeling about the knowledge and, for

some strange reason, a vision of some footprints on a beach. This scene stayed with me over the years, but I could never figure out what those footprints in the sand were supposed to mean.

In the meantime, of course, I have read your poem many times and have been touched by its profound meaning. I also became a Christian in the early 1970s.

It wasn't until just last year, however, during an extremely emotional crisis, that I was praying and happened to reflect upon the dream I'd had so many years ago. Again, the image of footprints in the sand appeared for just the briefest moment. What did it mean? And at that instant God answered my question. In a flash I realized the significance of your lovely poem "Footprints" to my dream. It was so obvious, but why had I not realized it before? As a young girl my Lord was warning me of a disaster to come—and that he would carry me through those difficult times ahead, just as he was carrying me at that very moment.

I cried and thanked the Lord for all the times He had carried me and then, in a simple request, I asked Him to provide me with a copy of the poem. And I thought, "Now, how is He going to do that?" The very same evening I picked up a book I had been reading, *Love Must Be Tough*, by Dr. James Dobson, and after reading a few pages, there before my eyes was the copy I'd requested of "Footprints."

I'm sorry you had to go through so much heartache about the poem, but it has been such a blessing to me that I feel as if the words of the poem came straight from the Lord God himself.

Sincerely,
Lorrissa
California

*

Dear Margaret:

"Footprints" has had a great effect on my life. It gave me strength during one particular incident in my life that I'd like to share with you.

It was March 10, 1991, when my fiancé and I were hit by a vehicle traveling at approximately seventy miles per hour. We were hit in the passenger side, and my feet were pinned beneath the wreck. Spitting parts of my teeth out while covered in blood, I was in shock. You see, it was my wedding year and I was to be married August 31, five and one-half months away. I suffered cracked ribs and a broken shoulder bone, lost some teeth, had a broken nose, and was scarred on my nose and chin. I also had the upper tissue in my gums severed, and to this day I still don't have any feeling there. I waited so long for the day that I would happily walk down the aisle, but now it seemed that this event would not take place for at least another year.

During this time, I pulled out my bookmark with "Footprints" on it. I kept crying and reading, crying and reading. The hope that God was carrying

me through this rough time in my life was the only
thought that kept me going. I was in so much pain,
both emotional and physical, that if my faith had not
been there, I could not have made it. Shortly after my
accident, my sister Mary, who suffered from mental
illness, had another nervous breakdown. Would my
wedding go as planned? Now I had physiotherapy, lots
of dental work to be done, family stress to cope with,
and a wedding to plan. I brought out "Footprints" so
many times during this period that it almost seemed
as if it was part of me.

My dental work was completed two weeks before
my wedding. The aches and pains were still there,
but my scars were covered with makeup. Though on
medication, my sister was at the wedding, and that is
what really mattered. The wedding went as planned,
and I owed it all to the encouragement I got from
"Footprints."

My feeling is that whenever tragedy of any sort hits you,
you need a way to deal with it. The best way I dealt
with it was through faith in God and faith that He was
with me all the way. I believed that God was carrying

me through this rough time in my life, and I knew that things would work out as long as I had faith in God.

The wedding was beautiful, and two months later I was expecting my daughter, who is now fifteen months old. "Footprints" is indeed a magnificent piece of work that those who believe in God—and even those who don't—can use to heal their wounds and to find great strength to overcome the obstacles or tragedies that come their way. It helped me tremendously, and that is why I have included it in my book, *The Key to Happiness*.

I am sure that there are many, many lives to whom this poem has given strength. I only hope that many more people will be affected by it as I have been. It will keep changing people's lives, for through it we find the courage to believe that God is watching over us and that He is guiding us and will carry us over the rough or bumpy roads.

Sincerely,
Michele
British Columbia

Dear Margaret and Dear Paul,
God bless you!

Maybe this letter is a little surprise for you.
But please, let me introduce myself: My name is
Rico. I'm 26 years old and I live in Germany. I live
with my parents in a small village. I have two great
sisters and one great brother. I'm a self-employed
person and I earn my money by drawing and
teaching drawing in workshops for children. It's
often not easy, but I love my work very much, and
God cares for me. I'm a Christian and I try to go
through my life in love to our God, to Jesus, and to
the Holy Spirit. I try to practice charity every day
toward the people around me. I think that's enough
about me for the moment. I hope you can understand my English. I think it isn't the best. Now you
know some facts about me. But why have I written
you a letter?

On Christmas Eve 2008, I received a very wonderful gift from my younger sister: a little box. On

top of it were these words: "Time for you—with 'Footprints in the Sand' by Margaret Fishback Powers"! In this nice little box was a very beautiful small book: *Footprints in the Sand: The True Story Behind the Poem That Inspired Millions.* How great and amazing was this gift? I would find out in the next days.

Dear Margaret, I have read your wonderful poem. Yes, it's true our Lord carries us so often in our life. He takes our hand, He takes our body, He takes our soul, and then we can see only one set of footprints in the sand. I'm very deeply touched in my heart. And then I have read the story about your poem, the touching story about the life of Margaret and Paul and their daughters. There I can see how the Lord helps you through life and shows you the right way. It's hard for me to describe what I felt when I was reading the story of your life.

With this letter I am sending you a photocopy of one of my paintings. It's called "The New Beginning." On the back I have written some personal words. I hope you like it and that this little gift brings you joy.

For the future I wish you all the best, lots of health for body, heart, and soul, much power and energy for new tasks and new ways, and of course many moments of joy. God protect you and bless you!

Again, all the best to you and also to your family!

With kind regards from Germany,
Rico
Cunewalde, Germany

*

Dear Margaret Fishback Powers:

Christian Greeting.

For my birthday, my friend gave me a book called *Footprints: Scripture with Reflections Inspired by the Best-Loved Poem*. I read my book every morning (devotions). It's nearly four years, and I enjoy it thoroughly.

I had a stroke eight-and-a-half years ago. I was only 57 years old. I'm now 65. I lost my husband, Jim, one year and three days after my stroke. The stroke was on my right side, and it affected my speech. I'm only partly paralyzed. After two years, the doctor gave me permission to drive my car.

My speech is coming back thanks to Janet, my tutor. I thank Janet and I thank the Lord. I'm determined, and I don't give up.

I bought a number of copies of *Footprints: The True Story Behind the Poem That Inspired Millions*. I mailed them to friends in Newfoundland, Nova Scotia, and here in Ft. McMurray, Alberta.

I gave Janet a copy as well. She is grieving for her
boyfriend, who died last February. I said that your
book will bring comfort—"in our sorrow, in our
loneliness, in the hard times." I also gave your book
to my friend Marie, who is grieving for her husband.
She told me that the book brought comfort to her
soul.

God spoke in my heart nearly four years ago. Your
book has brought comfort to me.
God bless you, your husband, and your family.

With love and prayers,
Marie
Ft. McMurray, Alberta

*

Dear Margaret,

Matthew and I wanted to share with you the many simple ways the "Footprints" poem has touched our lives.

I (Joyce) personally encountered this poem at a young age when I was given a Bible and the poem was glued to the title page and written with my name on it. I may not have fully understood the poem at that young age of four, but it was a poem that grew with me throughout my life.

As I journeyed through life, many times God would place it in my life to remind me that He is journeying "with" me. Even through tears of loneliness and a feeling of being unable to bear all that was laid on me to carry, I really cherished the reminder that He is there through it all. Thank you for writing this poem, and thank you for your humility in sharing it even while it was being published as an "Anonymous" work. Had Matthew not had the privilege of knowing the full story, we would not have had this chance to thank you personally. Also, thank you so much for attending our wedding. We are truly blessed to be reminded that this journey into our marriage is still a journey with Him as He walks with us and talks with us through it all.

As for me (Matthew), the poem has been an inspiration which reminds me that, to God, the journey is more important than the end result. Both Joyce and I keep the "Footprints" poem inside our graduation Bibles from Vancouver Chinese Presbyterian Church Preschool. I find the poem very helpful when speaking the truth that Jesus is always walking with us, even when it doesn't seem like it is so and, even more, that he carries us in our darkest hours. These are timeless truths. As well, they are truths that are especially important for our generation during these difficult times. Thanks, Margaret and Paul, for making a difference in our lives in so many ways—this poem being one of them. May God continue to bless you and your family.

In Christ,
Joyce and Matthew Wan
Vancouver

*

Hi Margaret,

Thank you for inviting me to share my thoughts
on your "Footprints" poem and to express how it is
relevant to young people.

When I was a teenager in Germany, I listened to a
Christian band sing a song about how God is carrying us during the tough times and not leaving us
to ourselves—although that is how we often feel.
The song was based on the "Footprints" poem, and
I personally was very touched by it. Of course, it
was nothing new to me. I already believed that God
never leaves us. There is, however, much more to it.
It is not only that God is with us when life seems
impossible. He is not just caring for us. He is carrying us. It goes so much deeper than a superficial "I
care about you." God loves us so much, and His love
has "hands and feet."

Your "Footprints" poem and books have touched
us and helped us to change many lives throughout

Germany, and we know that people love for you to visit and speak to us when you can.

In and For Him,
Michael and Priska
Richmond, British Columbia

*

Dearest Margaret,

It's a pleasure writing you this letter. I have your book *Footprints for Mothers and Daughters.* Every day I read its pages, which inspire me. I am from Cameroon, and this is my second year in Canada. I study public administration at university, but I am a lover of literature, and I read a lot in my spare time. Sometimes I write short poems and stories from childhood.

I was delighted when I saw this book and the author's name—Margaret, which happens to be my mother's name, too. I really cherish this book. I carry the book with me every day to school and read it on the bus. I sleep with the book on my bed, and sometimes after my studies, I read at least two pages before going to sleep. Some of the stories are very touching and help me to understand the importance of a mother. Sometimes I feel I'm seeing myself through the lives of the people in the stories.

I can't explain how I felt when I opened the book and found the story, "My Daughter, My Mentor." The author of that story shared her family's experience in Cameroon. It was just so overwhelming that I ran with joy to show my mom and couldn't wait to show my friends the next day at school.

I have a collection of books, and I always arrange them according to my favorite and most-read books. I originally had another book on top, but *Footprints for Mothers and Daughters* has replaced it. It is my favorite book ever.

Yes, I am very excited about reading your other "Footprints" books. Thank you for such a lovely and wonderful collection.

Yours sincerely,
Martina
Ottawa

Dear Margaret and Paul:

Thank you very much for your service to the Lord and to many people, including children, all over the world, through your ministries and writings. Your book "Footprints" has been published in Japan eight times since the first edition in October 1996, and I'm sure God uses "Footprints" to reach out and bring people closer to the Savior Jesus.

As you know, Japan was hit by a magnitude 9 earthquake in March 11, 2011. The members of Pastor Mori's church (Global Mission Chapel, Iwaki, Fukushima, Japan) and their friends have been tireless in their efforts to restore the destroyed areas. Do you remember when Pastor Akira Mori and Missionary Kjell Harjo took you to the beach in Iwaki, Fukushima? That beach was hit very hard by the tsunami.

May the Lord richly reward you for what you have done for His Kingdom, and may the seeds you have planted keep growing in children's hearts and souls.

With love and prayers,
Yoshie Matter
Japan

*

This letter and the following one represent the thoughts and deep emotions of longtime friends who have measured the worth of my life and my outreach to others. I believe their thoughts show hope for each of us as we move toward the future, no matter how difficult it may be at times. Each one of us has to take that all-important first step. It is surprising to know that people are watching our lives and what we have to offer them. We don't want to fall short of that measuring stick.

MFP

Hello Margaret Rose,

We have been thoroughly enjoying your newest release from HarperCollins—*Footprints for Mothers and Daughters*. While going through this book, we reminisced about my days with you at Tillsonburg High School, and the many fond memories we have of our two closely knit families.

A highlight for us has been seeing firsthand the impact that "Footprints" has had. Almost everywhere we have traveled over the years, we have experienced the poem's positive effect on such a diversity of lives.

My special reflection is the letter I wrote to the city fathers, recommending you for Tillsonburg's Favorite Son/Daughter award in June 2001 in recognition of your literary achievements. What a thrill it was to hear the announcement came that you were the first woman chosen.

We are encouraged every year by the many entries in the annual Footprints in the Sand Foundation poetry/prose contest in the local community and schools. When we have the Footprints Walk-a-thon ("Best Foot Forward for Others"), we are inspired that it is helping those, including members of our own family, who struggle with rheumatoid arthritis.

Margaret Rose, your God-inspired "I Had a Dream" (now better known as "Footprints") has been an inspiration and healing to our family and many of our friends. The nationality or culture of an individual doesn't seem to matter. The words are still spoken of with great awe and respect. Many people have said to us that the poem is such a "lifter-up" and such a joy.

Keep writing and sharing with the world. We need all the encouragement we can get! Best wishes from the both of us, the "other" Margaret Rose and Irv.

Irv and Margaret Rose Horton
Tillsonburg, Ontario

*

By way of introduction, my name is Trevor Newton, and I'm chairman of Paul's Little People's Ministry Association (PLPMA)—the board that provides direction to both Paul and Margaret Powers in their evangelistic ministry to children. I've come to regard Paul and Margaret as close personal friends, and I'd like to say a few words about the importance of "Footprints" to our board, to my family, and to me. (Before I begin, I should note that the board has nothing to do with the administration of any of the many aspects of Margaret's creative side—other than to be in awe of the inspiration she has been to so many people!)

Where do I start to describe the impact that "Footprints" has had? It has been profound! The highlight of a board meeting is hearing about the great contribution that the children's ministry has made to so many young people. Paul and Margaret would often share stories about those who have told them of the significance that "Footprints" has had on their lives . . . not realizing that Margaret was the author. It continues to amaze me (but it doesn't surprise me) that the poem is so popular and that it continues to deeply move so many people around the world. It was truly God inspired.

Along with the rest of the world, I too have sensed that I was sometimes alone during my various personal trials, only to realize that the Lord indeed was there with me and had carried me through. "Footprints" has helped me focus on what is important and has reminded me of His great love; and that He is indeed omnipresent. He is there for me whether I feel His presence or not. My wife, Chris, reminded me of the time when one of our daughters brought her a copy of the poem and asked if she would make a needlepoint of it to help our daughter through a low point in her life.

I am one of millions to be positively affected by this poem. The Lord has used Margaret Fishback Powers, and her poem, to provide a great blessing to people around the world. I would like to take this opportunity not only to thank Margaret for her wonderful blessings to us all but also to encourage her as she continues to build on the "Footprints" legacy.
With much Christian love and respect,

Trevor Newton
Chairman, PLPMA

*

The following tribute to my mother was written in 1998 and presented as the Mother's Day Conference Message at the J.O.Y. (Just Older Youth) Club, Blue Mountain Baptist Church, Coquitlam, British Columbia.

Footprints of Faith
Margaret Fishback Powers

Several weeks ago, I picked up cards at a Hallmark
store. I was under stress. I had made my own cards
until the day I married, and continued doing so
throughout the years as wife and mother. I felt that
I was the only one who could put together just the
right words for my loved ones. Now, I had suddenly
turned to store-bought cards. My tear-filled eyes
scanned Get Well, Birthday, Miss You, Baby Shower,
Congratulations, and Sympathy shelves. Then I spotted
a Mother's Day card that was beautiful and seemed
to say all the words I wanted to say to my mother.
However, it was too late. I showed it to my husband,
and he gently reminded me that my dear Mom didn't
need to read how we felt about her. She had passed on
to Glory only a few months previously. He told me
that my handmade cards probably meant more to her
than all these lovely store items.

As we reread the card, I wondered if I had shared all
these glowing tributes to her, face to face. Had I told her
how much I appreciated the hours she spent cooking
and trying to teach me to cook? How much it meant to

learn the importance of making a sudden surprise over-night guest feel comfortable and welcome in our home? She would always say, "Anyone can have a house, but it takes extra love and care to make it a home."

How I missed her encouragement and smiling face when I left for teachers' college and university. Then, when I left for northern Quebec, I really missed her. But she never failed to write, and I still have a beautiful box of her letters, with ribbons and bows to tie them up; her handwritten words give me comfort. I treasure the times spent with her—in the fields, hoeing; in the garden, weeding and chatting; or out in the barn, look-ing at newborn animals or gathering eggs. She would relate stories of her family history, of her parents, grandparents, and great-grandparents, and tell of those special talents they had been given, and their walk of faith.

Mom passed on "tales of a path well worn." She often said, "Just like women of the Old and New Testament, we too must walk by faith that new path ahead, and mark it well for those who follow by faith in our footprints."

It was not easy to follow in Mom's footprints of faith—footprints that she walked daily in the sight of the Lord. She was so consistent, so unconditionally loving to her family and friends, and faithful to her last day on Earth. Her trust was like a new piece of ground to be cleared, tilled, prepared, and seeded. She wanted a good harvest, and I believe her daughters have called her blessed, as we read in Proverbs 31:28.

I talked to my mom by telephone long distance a few hours before her going home, and if I had known that it was to be our last conversation, I would have kept her talking all night. I can't talk to her now, but I must try to transfer her recipe for a walk of faith to my daughters and granddaughters and let them know that Mom left deep footprints for us to follow.

*

The two remembrances that follow appeared in my recent book, *Footprints for Mothers and Daughters*. The authors are my two special daughters, whom you've met in the pages of *Footprints: The True Story*.

MODERN MUM, by Paula Callahan

I am a woman who has a healthy relationship with her
mother. I enjoy Mum's company and look forward to hanging out with her whenever possible. It is not too often, since
we live in different countries. We never measure distance
physically when we judge closeness of the heart and soul.

My parents were teacher-missionaries before I was
born, and they raised me while traveling the globe. I
was able to experience the many positive, and negative, situations that affected me, my parents, and the
church. God created the three of us to be optimistic.
This attitude has helped me to endure the distance
away from family yet cherish our times spent together.

I underwent no teenage rebellion. I took time to
learn to be a wife, a mom, and a strong woman, but
dependent on God. Mum taught me to deal with
kindness and bitterness, and to be content in all my
circumstances. The training helped me cope and deal
with very difficult and life-altering situations later on.

Mum's strong yet gentle hands have guided me
through many tough decisions—and sometimes she
would guide me by telephone from Great Britain,
Asia, Europe, or South America. I am thankful for our

close relationship. My girlfriends in North America are amazed, since some of them do not have an honoring, respectful, and warm friendship with their mothers. The mother-daughter bond needs to be nourished early in life, so that the connection is never severed and can continue in grandmother years. My mum is a modern grandmother. We call her "Nana." I am making every effort to foster the same wonderful kind of relationship with my daughter that I have had with my mum over my lifetime.

As a modern mum, I think like her, look like her, and act like her, although I don't enjoy heights, or zip-lining, or traveling (to countries lacking flush toilets). Don't get me wrong: I admire and respect my mother's courageous faith and love of adventure. I expect my daughter to understand her Nana, and not just think she is "cool" because she writes, travels, and zip-lines. As I strive to develop a similar relationship, I am beginning to realize the great effort it took my ever-busy mum to passionately, and persistently, place me near the top of her never-ending list of most important persons. I appreciate her positive efforts even more today, as I walk farther down the path that her friendship has been training me for all my life.

*

MEMORY BOOKS, by Tina Harback

When I was growing up, my family traveled a lot. My parents were in ministry, and we had many opportunities to visit different places. Before my parents were married, my mom had been a schoolteacher, and that experience served her well—she taught us during our travels.

Long before I ever heard of the idea of a travel journal, my mom had my sister and me filling in notebooks with daily entries of our adventures. When I see scrapbooking idea books now, I laugh to myself. My mom carefully and diligently documented every town, city, and country we visited. She kept plane tickets, menus, photos (of course), pamphlets, newspaper clippings—anything you could think of. Each trip had its own special book, with a running commentary on each page. I can look at trips from when I was six or seven years old and remember them in detail, thanks to the time and care that my mom took to keep those memories preserved. My children love to look through the books, too, so I am especially glad that Mom documented our travels so well.

Even though we don't travel as a family anymore, my mom and dad are still on the road most of the year. I love it when they return and share all their experiences with us, through photos, pamphlets, and little mementos. I have seen some beautiful scrapbooking journals —lovely lettering, background papers, stickers, and sayings. I appreciate all the time and effort that it takes to produce these keepsakes. Then I remember Mom and the wonderful, simple way that she catalogued our adventures, and I smile. They may not be professional works of art, but they are creative and detailed, and very personal.

I need to take a page from my mother and make some simple memory books—books that can be shared, enjoyed, and, hopefully, treasured as much as the ones my mom created.

*

Other Poems

Poetry has always been one of my most enjoyable pastimes. It is a form of communication. I write poetry and prose, and play the piano and organ, to relax and express my thoughts—or to deal with situations—or, sometimes, just to bring back memories from childhood.

I can't always explain the process, and I don't always understand why or how the words come to me. It's rather like a soft feather blowing in the wind, or a child's faint voice in the middle of the night. But it is a gift that has been given to me. In turn, I have shared it with others throughout my life. I call it "giving back," something I see increasing numbers of people doing today. We all have gifts to use wisely, whether it is writing the words or editing them to present to the world.

I wrote many poems before "Footprints" and have written many since. My readers have possibly been touched by it more than by any of the others, but they are all very important to me. I am pleased to share some of these other poems, and I hope you enjoy them.

Can You Measure a Child's Future?

The line of dots that runs up our wall
Tells us our child is growing quite tall;
Shoes that were large now squeeze her toes;
My, how quickly a little child grows.

We are so eager to keep track of her height,
In her physical growth we take such delight;
But spiritual growth, which to God is a treasure,
We might forget, and fail to measure.

More important than inches, or dots on the wall,
Is increasing in wisdom; as Jesus grew tall,
He grew in favor with God and with man.
Will your child do this? With your help, she can!

Author's note: As I reflect on this poem, which I wrote to remember our young daughter, I remember using a pen to make ongoing marks beside our patio door for her to see as she grew taller. That became a tradition not just for our children (as we moved from house to house) but for our grandchildren as well. Whenever we would meet with the grandchildren, in our home, at airports, or elsewhere, it was their great joy to "measure up" to see if they had passed Nana. I would ask my readers if it is now time to erase these marks of tradition and just enjoy the memory.

*

Mother's Prayer

Dear Lord,
May my children grow to be confident.
May they be healthy,
independent adults
caring for themselves
and reaching out to others.
May they have long, successful lives
that grow from failures and errors
I have allowed them to make.
May they have godly, helpful mates
and satisfying careers.
Give me peace and contentment,
and when time marches on,
help me let them go.

Author's note: This is as important a poem today as it was the day I wrote it, at a camp near Ottawa. In the fall of 2011, we again had to "release" our children and grandchildren as they moved on to a greater distance. Many of you go through this time of empty nesting. We'd prefer a "See you later" rather than "Good-bye!" We never know what is ahead, but we know who goes before us and prepares the way.

*

A Heart for Children

One hundred years from now
It will not matter
What kind of car I drove,
What kind of house I lived in
How much I had in my bank
Nor what my clothes looked like.

One hundred years from now
It will not matter
What kind of school I attended,

What kind of typewriter I used,
How large or small my church,
But the world may be
. . . a little better because . . .
I was important
in the life
of a child.

Author's note: This was my father's favorite poem. I wrote it in 1963 in Mount Elgin, Ontario. My father would often have me read my poems to him. He was a wise force in monitoring the long-term value of my work. He would say, "Do you want people to read that piece of poetry [or prose] when you become an adult? Would that piece of work last and be of benefit to the world, or should it go in File 13? Some of my best "critical essays" went into File 13 when I realized they were not my most excellent work and would not encourage or build up another person.

*

Tolerance

Could we only see the goodness
Of the ones we meet each day,
We would overlook their failures,
As we greet them on Life's way.

Help me be patient with others' faults;
I know they are patient with mine.

Author's note: We all need to practice tolerance, patience, and understanding. God is not finished with me. He is still working on me and will do so until I take my very last breath!

*

Take Time

Take time to work,
it is the price of success
Take time to think,
it is the source of power
Take time to play,

it is the secret of youth
Take time to read,
it is the foundation of knowledge
Take time to worship,
it is the highway to reverence
Take time to enjoy friends,
it is the source of happiness
Take time to live,
it is the one sacrament of life
Take time to dream,
it hitches the soul to the stars
Take time to laugh,
it is the support to lift life's load
Take time to pray,
it brings Christ close to you,
And washes life's dirt from your eyes.

Author's note: I trust you, as my reader, will take time to absorb my words and thoughts, will make them your "life lessons well learned," and will pass them on.

*

Broken Dreams

As children bring their broken toys
With tears for us to mend,
I brought my broken dreams to God
Because He was my friend.

But then instead of leaving Him
In peace to work alone,
I hung around and tried to help
With ways that were my own.

At last I snatched them back and cried,
"How can You be so slow?"
"My child," He said, "What could I do?
You never did let go."

Author's note: This is my special piece, written to remember a broken wooden doll cradle. It reminded me of how we don't give God a chance to answer our questions and needs but instead "snatch" them back from Him and make our own decisions. We need to wait for God.

*

What Is a Grandmother?

A grandma is someone special
Who kisses tears away,
Who always has some special treats
At the end of a busy day.
Who knows a thousand stories
And riddles, tricks, and rhymes
Of which her listeners never tire
Though heard a hundred times.
Yes, a grandma is real special
And there are very few
As loving, kind, and precious
Or as special, dear, as you.

Author's note: I wrote this poem at the age of thir-teen. It is about my "Grandma Great," who encour-aged my poetry.

*

The Golden Box

Once upon a Christmastime
Just thirteen years ago
Our little daughter taught Dad
Something he didn't know.
It happened when she got into
Some costly seasonal wrapper;
Its golden glow had caught her eye—
All heaven could not stop her
From covering her precious gift
With such a special find,
But when he saw what she had done
He nearly lost his mind.
He yelled at her and something more
For which he felt much shame,
He spanked and yanked that little girl,
Yet he was the one to blame
For getting mad and making things
More costly than they seem.
For what's more special than a child,
More fragile than her dream?
Christmas Day dawned crisp and clear
And gifts were all displayed,

With gleeful joy the golden gift
Into his hands was laid.

Author's note: The story behind this poem is told in Chapter 10.

*

Once, when I was struggling with the question of what makes me write, I shared my concern with my daughter Paula. She replied, "Mom, that's just who you are. But I will write a poem that will help to answer your question." Here it is. I think her wise words say it all and provide a fitting close to this book. They finally gave me peace of mind and the knowledge that, whether I realized it or not, I was passing this gift on to the next generation.

Freedom

Whatever else poetry is,
It is Freedom.
Freedom to express,
to live, to love.

And yet not all can
understand.
Not everyone sees into
the poet's eyes,
life, heart,
and can guess what chasing
havoc in the mists of
mind have forced
the poet to take up pen.
The urgent mist,
the fog that distorts
truth or lies,
will never burn off
in a poet.
The misting rain,
both tears and ocean spray
cling to the inside
of the poet's eyelids,
pouting on the ridge
of the lashes,
yearning for escape.
And so the poet
writes the poem,
and the poetry

is Freedom.
The poet sighs,
rests from the chaos of
thoughts
hiding and seeking in the
opaque air.
Soon,
though,
movement begins.
Images form.
Souls develop.
Love threatens.
And so the weary poet
picks up pen
and stares at
a white record
of thoughts,
and emotion.
And draws a picture,
through poetry.
But for the poet,
once again,
there is Freedom.

—Paula Margaret Powers

Acknowledgements

My thanks to Lillian White, my teacher, and her husband, Kenneth, both lifelong friends; Dr. Barry and Audrey Moore, friends and counselors over the years; Dr. Geoffrey Still, our mentor and confidant throughout our marriage years, and his wife, Beverly, and their family; Dr. Thomas and Susan Standlee and their family, for unconditional friendship; Jeannette Clift George, actress, supporter, and lifelong friend; and Fred and Elaine Burnett and Alma Frederick; Rev. John Ballard, for encouraging and promoting my work; Uncle Redd Harper, actor and singer, deceased February 1992; William Hendley, missionary, who was present on the

"Footprints" weekend; David and Cathy Smith, longtime friends; Trevor and Chris Newton and family; my husband, Paul, and dearest daughters, Christina Michelle and Paula Margaret.

Special acknowledgements to those who were involved with the original edition: Helen Jenkins, proofreader; Gena Gorrell, editor; the Kelly family; and Claude Primeau and Nancy Colbert. My sincere thanks as well to those involved with this new edition, including copy editor Judy Phillips and the staff at HarperCollins: Norma Cody (the first friendly voice you hear when you call or visit the office), Brad Wilson, Alexis Alchorn, Allegra Robinson, Noelle Zitzer, and Neil Erickson. I appreciate the expertise and good humor of Dan Liebman, who spent hours shaping this book.